Called to Prayer

An anthology of prayers for public worship and for personal use

Compiled by Maureen Edwards

Front cover image "Fool of God (Christ in the Garden)" by Mark Cazalet, from the Methodist Church Collection of Modern Christian Art, by kind permission of the Trustees of the Collection.

ISBN 1 85852 198 X

Printed by Stanley L. Hunt (Printers) Ltd., Rushden, Northamptonshire.

Called to Prayer

Contents

Preface

Prayer – together or alone – is an integral part of our calling to follow Christ. Without it we will neither grow in faith, nor find the energy we need to be his witnesses in the world. That is why this book takes up the current theme of the Methodist Church in Britain – 'Our Calling': our call to worship, to grow in faith and care for one another, to be good neighbours and to go out and make new followers.

These prayers have been offered by people from many different backgrounds, some from within the United Kingdom and some from our partners in other parts of the world. They invite us to pray alongside rural and urban communities worldwide and to share the faith, the suffering, the hopes and dreams of thousands of people in widely differing situations. We are to remember that prayer transcends the miles and geographical boundaries and the periods of historical time that separate us. Prayer draws us together into a living, worldwide community in the presence of God.

It is awe-inspiring to reflect on how such a variety of prayers weave together. That, I am sure, is the work of the Spirit. It is fascinating too to notice that not only do the prayers which come from our partners relate to the need for peace and justice but also to making followers, while Christians of the so-called 'developed world' focus more on adoration, pilgrimage and personal petition. I believe God may be saying something to us here.

Indeed, one of the ways God speaks to us today is through the prayers of others, and that is what makes a book like this so spiritually enriching and challenging. Many prayers actually inspire us to go out and share our faith with others and to do God's will in the world. They also make us think more deeply. As you use these prayers, think of the country or situation from which they come. Listen to what God may be saying to you from someone of another culture, or from another period of history, or from a personal experience that is different from yours. For prayer is about listening rather than presenting our needs to God. God is within us, beside us, all around us and already knows what we all need. For this very reason, we are to pray 'with' as well as 'for' others. There will be no magic cure for the issues that cause conflict and suffering in Northern Ireland, in many African countries, in the Holy Land, Sri Lanka . . . or in the sufferings we face as individuals but, together in prayer with God, we enter into these situations. Prayer is a way of expressing our solidarity with others in their need.

This selection of prayers comes mostly from the *Methodist Prayer Handbook* of the last ten years. It is a follow-up to *Oceans of Prayer* (NCEC, 1991) which was a collection of prayers used in the 1980s. We would like to express our deep appreciation to each of the writers and our hope that this book will become an invaluable resource both for personal prayer and for public worship.

Maureen Edwards

Note: Except where indicated, prayers come from the United Kingdom, though Ireland is given special mention.

I

Our Calling – Worship

1. Day by day

1. We stand today,
    a link in a chain of prayer
    joining us to every person
    who has ever prayed
    since time began.
    A pillar of prayer down the ages,
    arising from desert sands,
    from the words of patriarchs
    of many nations.
    Lord, hear our prayer.

    We join our prayers
    to those of our brothers and sisters
    in every part of the world,
    prayer offered in every language
    at every moment of the day.
    Lord, hear our prayer.

    Thank you, God of all time,
    God of all places,
    that you hear each prayer.
    Lord, hear our prayer.

    Diane Clutterbuck

2. I praise you, Father, for the peace of the night and the gift of the day. Teach me to accept both blessing and tribulation at your hand, for you make all things work together for good. Amen

Dietrich Bonhoeffer (1906-45)

3. Just for today, what does it matter, O Lord, if the future is dark? To pray for tomorrow I am not able. Keep my heart only for today, grant me your light – just for today. Amen

St Therèse of Lisieux (1873-97)

4. Open wide the windows of our spirits, O Lord, and fill them with your light. Open wide the door of our hearts, that there we may receive and entertain you with all the powers of adoration and love; through Christ our Lord. Amen

Christina Rossetti (1830-94)

5. Creator Spirit, come, visit every waiting mind, come, pour our joys on all creation, set us free from sin and sorrows, and make us worthy to be your temples. Amen

Mercy Amba Oduyoye, Ghana

6. Gracious God, Holy Trinity,
God above us, God below us, God around us,
blessed are you and worthy of all praise.
Teach us at this time to rely on your grace,
to trust in your mercy and to respond to your love,
that we may welcome the opportunities this day brings
and know the encompassing presence of your Holy Spirit
through Jesus Christ our Lord. Amen

John Taylor

7.   Help me, Lord, to remember that religion
     is not to be confined to church or closet,
     nor exercised only in prayer and meditation,
     but that everywhere I am in thy presence;
     so may my every word and action have a moral context.

Susanna Wesley (1669-1742)

8.   Lord, let me discern you with equal joy in times of
     business and in times of prayer. Let me know you with
     equal tranquillity in the noise and clatter of the kitchen
     and in the blessing of your holy sacrament; through Jesus
     Christ our Lord.

After Brother Lawrence (1611-91)

9.   Gracious God, in whose will is our peace, help us this
          day
     to discover your image in those whom we meet,
     to discern your presence in the rich variety
     of human experience, and to display in our lives
     the love of Christ our Lord;
     for your name's sake. Amen

Michael Townsend

10. Eternal God,
     make our spirits open to the moving of your Holy Spirit
     that, being in tune with you at all times,
     we may carry out your will
     each day of our lives. Amen

Bob Garner

11.   Lord God, who greets us anew
        in the change and challenge of each day,
        grant us insight to recognise you at work,
        stillness to hear you speaking to us
        through the events of this day,
        and courage to respond. Amen

Ian White

12.   Help us today, O Lord,
        to see something of the beauty of our fragile world
        and of your unbreakable love.

        So help us to live today with vigorous joy
        and proper care
        and unshakeable peace. Amen

Kenneth Hext

13.   My Lord, my God,
        I will seek you this day in silence and in words,
        in the street and in the church,
        in the immediate and in the strange,
        in work and in prayer.
        Help me not to be too surprised that when I find you,
        you are more beautiful than I had expected.
        And help me to discover
        that even when I have not searched for you,
        you have been searching out me. Amen

Stephen Plant

14.   Gracious God, whose love is wide enough to embrace all
        creation, yet close enough to be known in our deepest
        needs and personal joys, grant us grace to entrust this day
        and all it holds into your care. May your presence be our
        joy, our peace and our hope, through Christ our Lord.
        Amen

David Reddish

15. Lord Jesus Christ, who so often paused to talk with those you met on the way, save me from being so preoccupied with the tasks before me today that I have no time for the person on the edge of the crowd who is in need of my help, for the unexpected visitor who makes demands upon me, for the sudden emergency that interrupts my plans. Give me a right sense of priorities and the readiness to change them when need arises, yielding first place always to what love of you requires of me. For your name's sake. Amen

Pauline Webb

16. Thanks be to you, O God, that we have risen this day,
to the rising of this life itself.
Be the purpose of God between us and each purpose,
the hand of God between us and each hand.
The pain of Christ between us and each pain,
The love of Christ between us and each love.
Beloved of waifs, beloved of the naked,
**Draw us to the shelter-house of the Saviour of
the poor.**

The Iona Community

17. I go forth today
in the might of heaven,
in the brightness of the sun,
in the whiteness of snow,
in the splendour of fire,
in the speed of lightning,
in the swiftness of wind,
in the firmness of rock.
I go forth today
in the hand of God.

8th century Irish traditional

18. O God our Creator,
     Your kindness has brought us the gift of a new morning.
     Help us to leave yesterday,
     And not to covet tomorrow
     But to accept the uniqueness of today.
     (silence)

     By your love,
         celebrated in your Word,
         seen in your Son,
         brought near by your Spirit,
     Take from us what we need to carry no longer,
     So that we may be free again
     To choose to serve you
     And to be served by each other.

                                    The Iona Community

19. God of love, help us today
     to watch for you carefully,
     work for you simply,
     and rest in you gratefully,
     through Jesus Christ. Amen

                                    Christina Le Moignan

20. Lord, if this day you have to correct us
     put us right, not out of anger,
     but with a mother and father's love.
     So may we your children
     be kept from falseness and foolishness.

                                    Mexico (source unknown)

21. Gracious God, accept our gratitude –
     for the kindness of family and friends,
     for all the mercies of this day,
     for Sabbath rest and the beauty of worship,
     for the treasure that you have set within our earthen
         vessels.

     Forgive our lack of trust;
     forgive us when, like Mary of old, we cry out,
     'They have taken away my Lord
     and I do not know where they have laid him.'
     Forgive the harshness of our lives,
     the loudness of our personalities.

     And of your grace, grant us wisdom and vision,
     a loving heart and generous spirit.
     In all the activities of this coming week,
     the great and the small,
     the familiar and the strange,
     the beautiful and the commonplace,
     may we hold out trembling hands
     and touch but the hem of your garment
     and be made whole;
     through Jesus Christ our Lord. Amen

                                        Nigel Collinson

22. Thank you, Lord, for ordinary days;
     sunlight filling a room and tender colours of flowers in a
         bowl,
     the pattern of branches against the sky, and a blackbird's
         song;
     We thank you, Lord, for ordinary days.

                                          Honor Lloyd

23. Lord, take from us the wounds of yesterday,
     the stress of today,
     and fear of tomorrow.

                                        Source unknown

2. Adoration

24. Lord God, we come to you with hearts that are cold, that they may be warmed by your selfless love. We come to you with hearts that are sinful, that they may be cleansed by the Saviour's precious blood. We come to you with hearts that are weak that they may be strengthened by your Holy Spirit. We come with hearts that are empty that they may be filled with your divine presence, Father, Son and Holy Spirit. Amen

St Augustine of Hippo (354-430)

25. Help us, O God, never to fill the finite space between the divine and the human with anything less than yourself. Save us from all false absolutes and grant that we may find our consolation in you alone; wherein our finite lives are blessed with the infinity of your love; this we ask through Christ our Lord. Amen

Simone Weil (1909-43)

26. Fill up within us, O Lord, all that is wanting or lacking. Reform whatever is amiss and perfect the work which you have begun in us. Being made by you let us magnify you with our lips and being made for you let us glorify you with our lives; through Jesus Christ our Lord. Amen

John Wesley (1703-91)

27.   O God, beyond the reach of all thought,
we turn to you with finite minds.

Out of the vastness of eternity
we listen for the intimacy of your voice.
Though you are beyond all imagination
we long to gaze on your beauty.

In perfect silence
the heart of your divinity
speaks to the heart of our humanity,
love to love,
wounds to wounds.

Beyond the curving of space,
beyond the barrier of sound,
we encounter in your stillness
the centre of all our being.

O Glory, beyond all brightness,
O Love, beyond all telling,
O Wisdom, beyond all words,
we praise you,
we bless you,
we worship you,
Father, Son, and Holy Spirit, one God,
For ever and ever. Amen

Norman Wallwork

28.   Almighty God, your glory is beyond our understanding
and your love for all your creatures knows no limit; look
upon all your children in your mercy and deliver us from
our sins, sustain us in our temptations and bring us at the
last to your heavenly Kingdom; for to you, utterly good
and ever loving Father, Son and Holy Spirit, be glory for
ever and ever. Amen

John Sampson

29. Of your goodness, O God, give me yourself. In all things be my sufficiency. May I ask for nothing more and may I find you in all I want; for in you alone I put my trust, now and for ever. Amen

Julian of Norwich (c.1342-1416)

30. Lord Jesus Christ, pierce my soul with your love that I may long for you with my deepest desire and thirst for you, the source of all life, wisdom and light. May I seek you and find you, think on you and speak with you, and undertake all things for the honour and glory of your holy name; for your name's sake. Amen

St Bonaventure (1221-74)

31. Where are you to be found, O God?
How can I come
from my hurts and failures
to your holiness and majesty,
from my emptiness and despair
    to your mercy and love?
I dare not expect to know
    and feel your presence.
Yet my need is great
and your promise is for all.

In the depths
your love has found me, O God,
searched for me, and found me,
    and come within.
How can I describe my love for you –
    meeting my need with promises filled?
Your presence is real;
    I know it is true.
Accept my praise
and the whole of my life.

Jane Ashplant

32.   Help us, O Lord Jesus Christ, to enter into your sorrows
and to rejoice in your victory; to embrace your cross and
to wear your crown; to receive the wounds of your love
and to behold you in glory and light; for your own
name's sake. Amen

St Bridget of Sweden (1303-73)

33.   As the dew refreshes and cleanses fragile blades of grass,
as gentle rain feeds and lifts sun-dried leaves and
flowers,
and as the snow covers the earth and holds it
in frozen stillness,
so Lord, may we recognise your Spirit at different times,
answering our many needs,
challenging us to understand ourselves,
helping us to accept the waiting and stillness,
the moving and growing,
the resting and healing,
the planning and doing,
as constant stages of a journey with One
whose love holds us in each step.
God, in your goodness and endless generosity
we thank you that you are with us on the journey
and in the coming home.

Margaret Matta

34.   O God, most ancient and most new, food for eternity and
power of our being, you are inexhaustible in your love
and infinite in your glory. You are the source of all
goodness and fountain of all life. Draw near to us and
bless us with the glory of your presence that we may
worship you in spirit and in truth; through Christ our
Lord. Amen

John Henry Newman (1801-90)

35. O Lord our God, whose glory is above our understanding, whose mercy is without measure and whose love is beyond all telling; in your tenderness of heart look upon us and all whom we love, and deal with us according to the riches of your grace and compassion; through Jesus Christ our Lord. Amen

St John Chrysostom (c.347-407)

36. God of all bounty and goodness, whose work is life, whose love is grace and whose presence is glory; I call upon you with all my heart, I bless you with my whole being and I adore you, Father, Son and Holy Spirit, now and for ever. Amen

Lancelot Andrewes (1555-1626)

37. When we come to you, we find you have already come to us;
    you fill the silence and we hear your voice above the noise.
    We meet you in the peace and quiet of the soul
    and know your challenge in the pleading beggar.
    Help us not to turn our eyes from you,
    and make us glad in your presence.

Kenneth Hext

38. Prince of Peace,
    born in a stable and nurtured in a family, we adore you.
    Lord of Peace, healer of the sick,
    friend of the friendless and Saviour of all, we adore you.
    King of Peace, who died on a Cross
    and rose triumphant on the third day, we adore you.
    Lord Jesus, who said, 'My peace I give unto you',
    grant us grace to accept both Gift and Giver.

Edward Lacy

39.   You, O Christ, are the table set for all, the inextinguishable light of the saints; the sun shining in our midst, and you are joy and grace to your people.

Symeon the New Theologian (949-1022)

40.   Jesus, by your wounded feet, direct our path aright.
Jesus, by your nailed hands, move us to deeds of love.
Jesus, by your pierced side, cleanse our desires.
Jesus, by your broken heart, knit ours to yours.

Richard Crashaw (1613-49)

41.   O divine and glorious Trinity,
out of the fire of your mutual love
you brought the universe to birth.
In self-giving love
you have filled our lives
with your presence
that there your strength and gentleness
may be revealed.
You have made men and women
in your image,
called them to your side,
invited them into your garden
to share your covenant love.
In the days of our rebellion
you loved us in the voice of the prophets.
In the fullness of time
you have come to us yourself,
Love all-creating, Love all-redeeming,
Love life-giving.

With the warmth of your wings, shelter us,
and within the safety of your arms protect us;
both in the life that you share with us here
and in the glory that we shall share with you hereafter;
and this we ask for your name's sake.

Norman Wallwork

42. Lord Jesus Christ, whether in the quietness of my own resting place or in the busy storms of the day, amidst all the cares and joys of life, may I never feel forsaken or alone. Of your grace draw me entirely to yourself, now and for ever. Amen

Soren Kierkegaard (1813-55)

43. Lord Jesus, let me know you and let me know myself. Let me love myself as you love me. Let me fly to you, fear you and cleave to you. Call me to yourself and possess me now and for all eternity. Amen

St Augustine of Hippo (354-430)

44. Loving God, give us richness of imagination
to see you in the faces of everyone we meet,
so that we may adore and worship you unceasingly
and enjoy you as we enjoy other people;
through Jesus, lover of all.

Donald Frith

45. Coral reefs are both beautiful and dangerous;
the channels to negotiate are often narrow.
May we be aware of God's presence
where storms challenge us,
and may our eyes see the signs God intends us to follow.

Michael King

46. Grant to us in our prayers, Lord God, the gift of insight
that we may harvest passing thoughts
and set free imprisoned ideas,
for the good of your Kingdom. Amen

John Taylor

47. Saviour, teach me the silence of humility,
    the silence of wisdom,
    the silence of love,
    the silence of perfection,
    the silence that speaks without words,
    the silence of faith.
    Lord, teach me to silence my own heart
    that I may listen to the gentle movement
    of the Holy Spirit within me
    and sense the depths which are of God.

    Source unknown, 16th century

48. Creator God, who moves over water
    and brings boundaries out of chaos,
    Come to us.
    Redeemer God, who turns water into wine
    and enriches a marriage,
    Come to us.
    God of inspiration, who gives water to the tree of life
    and leaves for healing nations,
    Come to us. Amen

    Malcolm Braddy

49. **Come, Lord Jesus, make yourself known to us this
    day.**
    Thou shalt know him when he comes
    Not by any din of drums
    Nor the vantage of his airs
    Nor by anything he wears.
    Neither by his crown
    Nor his gown.
    For his presence known shall be
    By the holy harmony
    Which his coming makes in thee.

    Anon, 15th century

3. Praise and Thanksgiving

50.   Is not sight a jewel? Is not hearing a treasure? Is not speech a glory? O my Lord, pardon my ingratitude and pity my dullness who am not sensible to these gifts. The freedom of thy bounty hath deceived me. These things were too near to be considered. Thou presented me with thy blessings, and I was not aware. But now I give thanks and adore and praise thee for thy inestimable favours.

Thomas Traherne (1636-74)

51.   Great, O Lord, is your power and infinite is your wisdom; therefore we bless you without ceasing and delight in your praise. You have made us for yourself and our hearts are restless until they find their rest in you. Amen

St Augustine of Hippo (354-430)

52.   Blessed be God who has redeemed the world;
Blessed be God who came to bring riches to humankind;
Blessed be God who causes creation to resound with
       praise;
Blessed be God who welcomes the hosannas of pilgrims
and the alleluias of the saints. Amen

Ephraim of Edessa (c.306-373)

53. Eternal and most loving God: we thank you
        for your love and care,
        for your goodness and kindness,
        for your guidance and protection,
        for your Son, our Lord and Saviour,
        and for the Holy Spirit, who continues
        to make intercession for us.
     Grant that our hearts may grow
     in praise and thankfulness,
     that we may truly give all that we are and have
     to the honour and glory of your precious name. Amen

Lesley G Anderson, Panama

54. Holy, holy, holy, perfect Lord of Hosts,
     heaven and earth are full of the holiness of your glory.
     You have created all creatures with your word.
     You carry them all without being weary,
     and feed them all without ceasing.
     You think about them all without forgetting any.
     You give to all without being diminished.
     You water the earth without running dry.
     You watch over all without sleeping.
     You hear us all without neglecting any.
     While your presence fills every place,
     they have told us about you in a way we can receive.

Ethiopia

55. For rebirth and resilience, blessed be God.
For hunger and thirst to see right prevail, glory to God.
For all who speak out for the truth, let us praise the Lord.
For all who triumph over their bitter conditions, Alleluia.
For all who risk their lives and reputations for the gospel,
thanks be to God!

South Africa

56. Thank you, Father, for all those who struggle for peace,
justice and the dignity of their fellow human beings.

Thank you, Spirit of God, for the many people who use
their time and their resources to help those who suffer,
are persecuted, in need, oppressed, without hope.

Thank you, our Lord Jesus Christ, because you walk with
us through these difficult times, and show us that the last
word on the future of the world is your resurrection.
Amen

Claudio Martelli, tr. Jan Sutch Pickard

57. Lord, for the power to be gentle, for the strength to
forgive, for the patience to understand, for the endurance
that holds on to what is right, for the good that overcomes
evil, for the vision of a new world arising from the ruins
of the old, we give thanks and pray. Amen

Donald Eadie

58.   Worthy of praise from every mouth,
of confession from every tongue,
of worship from every creature,
is thy glorious name, O Father, Son, and Holy Ghost:
who didst create the world in thy grace
   and by thy compassion didst save the world.
To thy majesty, O God, ten thousand times ten thousand
bow down and adore, singing and praising without
   ceasing and saying,
Holy, holy, holy, Lord God of hosts;
Heaven and earth are full of thy praises;
Hosanna in the highest.

Nestorian (5th century)

59.   May none of God's wonderful works keep silence, night
or morning. Bright stars, high mountains, the depths of
the seas, sources of rushing rivers: may all these break
into song as we sing to Father, Son and Holy Spirit. May
all the angels in the heavens reply: Amen, Amen, Amen.
Power, praise, honour, eternal glory to God, the only
Giver of grace, Amen, Amen, Amen.

Source unknown (3rd-6th centuries)

60.   Lord, you have given so much to me. Give me one thing
more – a grateful heart. Not thankful only when it
pleases me, as if your blessings have sparse days. Grant
me a heart whose pulse may be your praise.

George Herbert (1593-1633)

61.   Give grace, O Lord, not only to hear thy Word with our
ears, but also to receive it into our hearts and to show it
forth in our lives; for the glory of thy great name.

Source unknown

62.   Lord, your glory fills the world
       and is seen in the life and work of all people.
       You are present in the experience
       and cultural heritage of all races.
       You inspire our use of colour, sound and movement
       and the rich resources of the earth.
       You made us in your image
       and gave us your creative ability.
       Thank you, Creator and Provider of all.

       Thank you for gifts of communication,
       speech and language;
       for the art of storytelling,
       enabling us to pass on traditions
       from one generation to another;
       for the gift of writing
       and the enrichment of mind
       that comes from the literature,
       poetry and wise sayings
       of people of many countries and periods of history.
       Thank you, Creator and Provider of all.

       Thank you for the gifts of dramatic art,
       the development of radio and television
       and the wealth of talent from many cultures
       they bring into our homes.
       Thank you, Creator and Provider of all.

       Thank you for varieties of sound and rhythm
       and the power of music and dance
       to make us forget ourselves
       and become one with the community.
       Thank you, Creator and Provider of all.

       Thank you for works of art and architecture,
       woodcarvings and sculpture,
       beautiful jewellery and ornaments,
       and the fashioning and design
       of clothes and textiles.
       Thank you, Creator and Provider of all.

Thank you for the gift of knowledge
and the development of science;
that we can look through microscopes
at the smallest units of your creation
and discover wonders invisible to the naked eye;
for the use of radiation
in the diagnosis and treatment of disease;
for new methods of agriculture
to combat soil erosion,
cultivate deserts
and provide food for everyone.
Thank you, Creator and Provider of all.

Maureen Edwards

63. **Thank you for music**
Lord, I thank you that you have spoken to us
in the music of words and melody,
in so many marvellous instruments,
in unison, and in harmony;
thank you for songwriters and musicians,
for bands, groups, and orchestras.
Sometimes, Lord, I hear sounds that speak of heaven:
I am 'lost in wonder, love and praise'.
How good it is to sing your praises,
to know you bless creativity,
that you speak in the music of life,
and that so many kinds of music can tell of you.
May we honour you in the music we sing.
May we praise you always with words and thoughts
    that are honest and true.
May we for ever sing Hallelujah!
May our shout be Hallelujah!

Tony Jasper

64. Loving Creator,
     We recognise you in a baby's eyes,
         And smile before we have thought;
     We hear you in a child's cries,
         And feel your pull in our heart;
     We know your delight in children's jokes and laughter,
         And relax in their spirit of joy.

     Thank you for the children in our churches.
         We love them in your name.
     Thank you for JMA and all children's workers,
         Who learn, pray and serve
             with your worldwide Church.
     Thank you for the child in us,
         Who knows you as Mother and Father
         and enjoys your smiles, your tears, your laughter
         and your love for us all. Amen

                                             Steve Pearce

65. God our Father, we offer thanks and praise for all you
     have done, all you are doing and all you will for us, for
     the Church and for the world. You have brought us into
     being. You are moulding us into your likeness, and you
     lead us forward into the light of your presence. By the
     power of the Holy Sprit, living and working in us, lead us
     to reflect your glory in the world, for the sake of Christ,
     your Son and our Saviour. Amen

                                             Morwenna Bennett

66. **A Chinese Grace**
     Each time we eat,
     May we remember God's love.

67. Lord of grace and beauty,
     we praise you that we glimpse your love
     in mountains and lakes,
     in trees and hillsides,
     in the wonder of nature,
     and the skill of human hands.
     Keep our eyes and hearts
     always open to this love.
     Through Jesus Christ our Lord. Amen

Donald Frith

68. Our Lord Jesus Christ,
     we express our thanksgiving for your love at all times,
     for your goodness,
     the blessings of peace
     and hope for the future.
     You alone are God.
     You alone are the provider of rain to water our crops
     and sunshine for our harvest.
     Bless your Church and all its leaders
     for your name's sake. Amen

Charles King, The Gambia

69. Almighty God,
     you are more ready to give
     than we are to receive,
     more ready to bless
     than we are to be blessed;
     grant us to know your gifts and your blessings
     in Jesus Christ our Lord,
     and to live both thankfully and generously,
     for his name's sake. Amen

Alan Horner, Scotland

4. Celebrating God's love

70. Lord, before ever you made us, you loved us. Nor has your love ever slackened, nor ever shall. In love all your works have been begun, and in love they continue. In this love our life is everlasting, and in this love we shall see you and be glad in you for ever. Amen

Julian of Norwich (c.1342- 1416)

71. O Love most powerful, strengthen me. O Love most sweet, let me taste your goodness. O Love most dear, let me live for you alone. O Love most faithful, comfort and support me. O Love most companionable, accompany all my deeds. O Love most victorious, persevere with me to the end; for your own name's sake. Amen

Gertrude of Helfta (1256-1302)

72. Set our hearts on fire with love for you, O God, that in its flame we may love you with all our hearts, with all our minds, with all our souls, and with all our strength, and our neighbours as ourselves; and grant that in the keeping of your commandments we may glorify you, the giver of all good gifts; through Christ our Lord. Amen

Orthodox Kontakion

73. Lord, fill us with the joy of your great love; let our minds meditate on it, let our tongues speak of it, let our hearts love it, let our minds preach it, let our souls hunger for it, and let our whole being desire it, until we enter into your glory and see you face to face. Amen

St Anselm (1033-1109)

74. Care for us, O Christ, with your tenderness; clothe us with your humanity; guide us with your gentleness; rule us with your wisdom; and exalt us with your love; for your mercy's sake. Amen

St Mechthild of Magdeburg (c.1210-80)

75. O Lord God, my All in all, Life of my life and Spirit of my spirit; look in mercy upon me and so fill me with your Holy Spirit that my heart shall have room only for that love which is of you and from you; for ever and ever. Amen

Sadhu Sundar Singh (c.1889-1929)

76. Gracious and compassionate God,
 you are the source of our being.
 In company with all your people around the world,
 help us that we may grasp 'what is the breadth and length
 and height and depth of Christ's love,
 and to know it, though it is beyond knowledge'
   (Ephesians 3:18,19).
 Fill us with all your fullness
 that we may live by that same love,
 reaching out spontaneously
 to all who need our presence and help.
 Strengthen the Churches of the world
 that we may grow in unity and love,
 reflecting your oneness, Father, Son and Holy Spirit.
   Amen

Israel Selvanayagam, Church of South India

77. Almighty and most loving God,
     We acknowledge your overflowing love
         and infinite glory.
     Purify our hearts.
     Teach us how to love and forgive.
     Pour down on us the spirit of peace and reconciliation.
     Challenge us to go out in service:
         to transform the world through self-renewal,
         to transform suffering into commitment,
         to transform confusion into creativity,
         to transform death into life.
     Teach us how to proclaim the good news:
         that we may be instruments of justice,
         committed to peace and equality for all.
     Teach us your people how to survive amid
         death by starvation,
         misery and destitution,
         torture and disappearances.
     Lord, sometimes our faith trembles.
     Lord, sometimes it seems as if you have left us.
     Lord, help us to trust you more
     and to put our lives into your hands!
     O God of unceasing love,
     To you be honour, glory and praise. Amen

                              Lesley G Anderson, Panama

78. O God, Creator of all peoples,
     grant us your strength of love
     that we may live with a vulnerable openness to each
         other
     which welcomes our diversity and difference
     as your gifts.

                              Will Morrey

79.　Deepen within us, holy and blessed Jesus, a true sense of your infinite love; that adoring you and believing in you, we may trust in your infinite merits, imitate your holy example, obey your wise commandments and finally enjoy your promises; for you live and reign with the Father and the Holy Spirit, one God now and for ever. Amen

John Wesley (1703-91)

80.　God of love, give us love:
Love in our thinking and our speaking;
Love in our doing and in the hidden places of our souls;
Love of our neighbours far and near;
Love of those we find it hard to bear
and of those who find it hard to bear with us;
Love in joy,
Love in sorrow;
Love in life and love in death.

William Temple (1881-1944)

81.　Lord, your love makes us and remakes us, again and again and again. Such love, in any situation, enables us to discover for ourselves that 'You are able to do exceeding abundantly above all that we ask or think, according to the power that is at work within us.' Amen

Kenneth Wilson

82.　Today, O Lord,
may we see with love's discernment
and serve with love's simplicity,
knowing that we are loved by you
in Jesus Christ. Amen

Christina Le Moignan

28

83. We bless you that we were made to love, as the stars were made to shine. Grant that such love may never die within us, but being daily rekindled in our souls, may burn in our hearts and for ever renew our whole being with the gift of eternal life; this we ask through Christ our Lord. Amen

Florence Allshorn (1887-1950)

84. Choreographer divine,
you danced creation into being
and call us to partner you in the dance.
Teach us the steps of faith;
whether our life be in quick step or slow,
may we be in tune with the rhythm and flow of your
  dance.
When we twist and turn in the dark places of our lives,
and discouragement and despair trip us,
hold us gently in your arms
and lift us in an arabesque of love and hope.
As we dance to unknown places and new opportunities
may we encourage others not just to tap their feet,
but to risk joining in the dance of life. Amen

Stella Bristow

85. Living God,
as we see your glory in the grandeur of the mountains
and in the beauty of the lochs,
help us to seek that same glory
in the meanest streets of our cities.
Enable us to walk there with you
that we may find the breadth, height and depth
of your love for all in Jesus Christ our Lord. Amen

Alan Anderson

86.   Lord God, out of Africa come many negative images.
        Droughts can be followed by floods;
        coups and counter-coups are commonplace;
        images of ethnic strife and tribal violence
        and all too familiar pictures of illness, malnourishment
        and infant mortality come into our homes.
        You know about this, Lord,
        for you are at the sharp end of these afflictions.
        You share in the totality of Africa's other images.
        Wise and loving Lord,
        remind us of Africa's other images.

        Every Sunday, millions throughout the continent
        dance before you, celebrating new life in Christ.
        You are the occasion of this joy, hope and love.
        Help us to learn from Africa how to celebrate you.
        Out of Africa's Church comes a witness
        to challenge the jaded cynicism of our age.
        Help us to learn from Africa how to celebrate you.
        Out of Africa's Church comes encouragement
        to hope in things unseen,
        to affirm the reality of the spiritual.
        Help us to learn from Africa how to celebrate you.
        Out of Africa's Church comes the witness
        of setting aside the hurts and oppressions of yesterday.
        Save us from being captive to our yesterdays;
        to learn how to pardon because we are greatly pardoned,
        and to love because we are greatly loved.
        Help us to learn from Africa how to celebrate you.

Brian Brown

87.   God, in Christ, you open yourself to us in love.
            Open our eyes, to see your beauty in human living;
            Open our ears, to hear your word in human speaking;
            Open our hearts, to love you in others.
        So may we find joy and fulfilment in you.

Graham Carter

5. Confession

88. I was slow to love you, Lord,
     your age-old beauty is still as new to me:
     I was so slow to love you!
     You were within me,
     yet I stayed outside
     seeking you there;
     in my ugliness I grabbed at
     the beautiful things of your creation.
     Already you were with me,
     but I was still far from you.
     The things of this world kept me away:
     I did not know then
     that if they had not existed through you
     they would not have existed at all.
     Then you called me
     and your cry overcame my deafness;
     you shone out
     and your light overcame my blindness;
     you surrounded me with your fragrance
     and I breathed it in,
     so that now I yearn for more of you;
     I tasted you
     and now I am hungry and thirsty for you;
     you touched me,
     and now I burn with longing for your peace.

     St Augustine of Hippo (354-430)

89. In our infirmity, O Lord, we come to the divine
     Physician; in our blindness to the radiance of eternal
     light; and in our sinfulness to the fountain of mercy.
     With purity of faith and in penitent love we pray for the
     gift of salvation; through Christ our Lord. Amen

St Thomas Aquinas (c.1225-74)

90. God of all grace,
     you are the refuge of those who fly to you
     and the hope of those who call upon you.
     Cleanse us from every thought which offends your
         goodness,
     refresh our souls and our bodies
     and purge our hearts and our consciences;
     that, with purity of heart
     and serenity of mind,
     we may come boldly and fearlessly
     into your holy presence;
     through Christ our Lord. Amen

Coptic Liturgy of St Basil

91. Almighty God, we confess before you
     and before one another
     that we have broken your laws
     and forgotten our promises;
     we have been thoughtless in our actions
     and we have wasted your gifts;
     we have neglected opportunities for good
     and we have gone our own way;
     we pray to you for forgiveness.

Norman Wallwork

92.   Forgive my sins, O Lord;
       the sins of my present and the sins of my past,
       the sins of my soul and the sins of my body,
       the sins I have done to please myself
       and the sins I have done to please others.
       Forgive my casual sins and my deliberate sins,
       And those sins I have laboured to hide even from myself.
       Forgive me, O Lord.
       Forgive all my sins, for Jesu's sake. Amen

Thomas Wilson (1663-1755)

93.   Take from us, O Lord,
       the spirit of laziness and half-heartedness,
       the spirit of selfish ambition and idle talk;
       and grant to your servants
       the spirit of integrity and purity of heart,
       the spirit of faithfulness and love;
       and the spirit of humility.
       This we ask for your mercy's sake. Amen

Orthodox Liturgy for Lent

94.   Gracious God,
       we confess that we have sinned against you,
       in thought, word and deed.
       We have not loved you with our whole heart and soul,
           with all our mind and strength,
       and we have not loved our neighbours as ourselves.
       We pray that you will forgive what we have been,
       help us to amend what we are,
       and direct what we shall be.
       May your goodness be ever first in our hearts
       and to our life's end may we follow in the steps of Christ
           our Lord. Amen

John Hunter (1849-1917)

95.   Great God and Father,
       as we call Gethsemane to mind
       our hearts are filled with penitence.
       Forgive our indifference to the cross,
       pardon our idle curiosity at the piteousness of the scene,
       help us to live anew
       and grant to us all a longing to be born again;
       through Christ our Lord. Amen

Toyohiko Kagawa, Japan (1888-1960)

96.   Lord Christ,
       for the tears shed in your infancy,
       pardon our sins of weakness.
       For the tears shed at the grave of Lazarus,
       pardon our sins of habit.
       For the tears shed over Jerusalem,
       pardon our sins of evil intent.
       For the tears shed in your passion,
       pardon our sins of wilfulness,
       and all for your love and your mercy's sake. Amen

Source unknown

97.   Look upon me, O Lord, with those eyes of love
       with which you looked upon Mary at the feast,
       upon Peter in the hall of judgement
       and at the dying thief upon the cross;
       and looking forgive:
       For like Mary, my love is great,
       like Peter, you know that I love you,
       and like the thief, I pray that you will remember me
            when you come into your Kingdom;
       for your love and your mercies' sake. Amen

Lancelot Andrewes (1555-1626)

98. We give ourselves to you, O God, to be emptied of all that is not of you. Cleanse us from all unrighteousness and, according to your will, take our hands and use them for your glory; through Christ our Lord. Amen

Dorothy Kerin (1880-1963)

99. Forgive us, O Lord, when we listen, but do not hear; when we look but do not see; and when we feel, but do not act, and by your mercy and grace draw us into the righteous deeds of your Kingdom of justice and peace; through Christ our Lord. Amen

Maria Hare (1798-1870)

100. Lord God,
we bring to you our sins
for your forgiveness,
our temptations for your strength
our sickness for your healing
and our loved ones for your protection;
through Christ our Lord. Amen

The Church in Kenya

101. God of compassion,
in whom grace is certain,
mercy ever flowing
    and peace deep stillness,
we confess our sin:
we are slow to trust,
have no longing to forgive
and we fail to notice the holy
    in your world.
Speak of your love,
that we may live in your freedom.
Touch us with healing,
and we will be whole.

Philip Turner

102.　God of truth and grace,
we find your truth hard to face,
especially when your light shines into our lives,
showing up our false values,
our self-deception and the lies we live.
When we fall from grace – **Forgive us.**

God of faith and hope,
we confess we have not kept faith –
so often we have given in to cynicism and despair;
we are so busy that we have no time
to reflect on what we believe,
or to sit at your feet and learn;
when we meet as a church,
sometimes our full agenda has no space
for the hope of the world.
When we fall from grace – **Forgive us.**

God of love and new beginnings,
we hurt each other – and you bring healing;
we break our promises – and you still believe in us;
we deny you – and you are still there.
When we fall from grace – **Forgive us.**

Our words are your crown of thorns,
our actions nail you to the cross –
and you say, 'Father, forgive,
for they do not know what they are doing.'
When we fall from grace – **Forgive us.**

We bury you, and you roll away the stone;
we meet you, and we are still uncertain;
we recognise you, and the next thing we know
you are blessing and sending us far and wide
to share the good news of your truth and love.
So, forgiven, may we go out from here,
to serve with love and share your grace.　Amen

Jan Sutch Pickard

103. Eternal and most gracious God: we confess that
             we have esteemed ourselves better than others,
             we have refused to help those who need us most,
             we have closed our gates on the poor and oppressed,
             we have ignored the cries of hurt and pain,
             we have forgotten to feed the hungry,
             we have neglected the homeless,
             we have not cared for the naked,
             we have lived for ourselves,
             obsessed with race, colour and nationality.

      O God, in your mercy
             forgive our sin,
             free us from pride,
             give us humility in all our relationships,
             and grace to choose your will.

      O God, in your love
             consecrate us anew for your mission,
             that we may go in faithfulness,
             and the assurance of your love,
             through Jesus Christ our Lord. Amen

Lesley G Anderson, Panama

104. Lord, today you made us known to friends we did not
      know,
      And you have given us seats in homes which are not our
      own.
      You have brought the distant near,
      And made a brother of a stranger,
      Forgive us, Lord . . .
      We did not introduce you.

Polynesia

105. Lord, you return gladly and lovingly to lift up the one
      who offends you and I do not turn to raise up and honour
      the one who angers me.

St John of the Cross (1542-91)

106. Let us pray for others . . .
      Let us pray for those who bind heavy burdens, hard to
        bear . . .
      Forgive, Lord, our moralising
      as we pray for those who try to live by the law,
      that they may experience your superabundant grace.
      Silence
      Lord, in your mercy,
      Hear our prayer.

      Let us pray
      for those who love places of honour at feasts
      and the best seats in the synagogue . . .
      Forgive, Lord, our selfish ambition
      as we pray for those who have no power,
      who have lost even the desire to hold out their hands,
      that they may find their purpose in your service,
      Silence
      Lord, in your mercy,
      Hear our prayer.

      Let us pray
      for those who love salutations in the market place . . .
      Forgive, Lord, our constant drawing of attention to
        ourselves
      as we pray for those who are ignored,
      that they may know that they are loved by you.
      Silence
      Lord, in your mercy,
      Hear our prayer.

      Let us pray
      for those who cleanse the outside of the cup and the
        plate,
      but inside are full of extortion and rapacity.
      Forgive, Lord, our impure desires
      as we pray for the victims of human greed,
      that they may receive their rightful share of your bounty.
      Silence
      Lord, in your mercy,
      Hear our prayer.

Let us pray
for those who are whitewashed tombs
    full of the bones of the dead . . .
Forgive, Lord, our readiness to judge by appearances
as we pray for those whose inner beauty outshines
    all outward show.
Silence
Lord, in your mercy,
Hear our prayer.

Let us remember the sick, the lonely and the bereaved . . .
Silence
Lord, in your mercy,
Hear our prayer.

Father, we give you thanks
that as we stretch out our hands,
you meet us in our need.
Touch us now and make us whole,
through Christ our Lord. Amen

John Taylor – G
Based on Matthew 23

107. Our Father in heaven, I thank thee that thou hast led me
into light. I thank thee for sending the Saviour to call me
from death to life. I confess that I was dead in sin before
I heard his call, but when I heard him, like Lazarus, I
arose. But, O my Father, the grave clothes bind me still.
Old habits that I cannot throw off, old customs that are so
much a part of my life that I am helpless to live the new
life that Christ calls me to live. Give me strength, O
Father, to break the bonds; give me courage to live a new
life in thee; give me faith to believe that, with thy help, I
cannot fail. And this I ask in the Saviour's name who has
taught me to come to thee.

Taiwan

108. God, merciful and gracious,
      You breathed life into all beings;
      You blessed us with minerals and waters
      As well as fruits and flowers and
      Beautiful living creatures great and small.
      We confess our faults and those of the world.
      Your Son Jesus gave us peace but
      We chose to divide ourselves and
      Hold on to values of this broken world:
      We waste the land and pollute the seas.
      Fear and prejudice set us against other beings;
      We discriminate on the basis of race;
      We violate your image in those we dislike;
      We oppress others and refuse them freedom;
      We are prisoners of our racism, oppressions
          and xenophobia.

      Creator God of heaven and earth,
      The Icon of justice, peace and creation,
      Help us to love each other as you loved us.
      Teach us to share the earth and
      To live in harmony with all who inhabit it. Amen

Naboth Muchopa

109. Loving God, you call us to love you with our whole
          being,
      but we respond by offering only a small part of our lives.
      In Christ you showed us how to put ourselves last,
      but we are still self-centred,
      insensitive to the needs and expectations of others.
      In the death of Christ you suffered for our redemption,
      but we turn back again and again
      to the ways from which you set us free.
      Forgive us, heal us,
      and love us into a deeper devotion to you
      and a stronger faithfulness to the ways of your Kingdom.
      In the name of Christ. Amen

Maureen Edwards

110. Gracious God, Creator of all things,
    we confess to you that we have squandered the gift of
        life,
    and we are at the precipice of self-destruction.
    We have allowed the unfettered drive
    toward profit and consumerism
    to determine the future of our own nations
    and international relationships.
    The good life of some is built on the pain of many;
    the pleasure of a few on the agony of millions.
    Come now into our lives
    and teach us anew that all created things are closely
        related
    and derive benefit from each other.
    Fill us with your wisdom,
    that we may grow in grateful enjoyment
    of your abundant creation,
    and safeguard the earth and seas for all generations
    to the honour and glory of your name, now and for ever.
    Amen

Akuila Yabaki

111. Creator, Son and Spirit,
    One God in perfect community,
    Look on us who look to you
    And hear our prayer for this community.

    Where there is any falseness,
    smother it by your truth.
    Where there is any coldness,
    kindle the flame of your love.
    Where there is any resentment,
    show us the road to compassion.
    Where there is anything we will not do for ourselves,
    make us discontent until it is done.
    And make us one
    as you are one.

The Iona Community

II

Our Calling – Learning and Caring

1. Church Life

112. Dearest Lord, whose glory is made no greater by our creation and whose power is made no stronger by our redemption; teach us to care for one another, not out of duty but out of love, and to be moved in all our actions by love and love alone. Amen

St Catherine of Siena (c.1347-80)

113. Living God, in all our dealings with one another today,
make us aware of each other as people,
with different personalities, needs and abilities.
Help us never to resent those who are doing better
     than we are,
nor to ignore those who are quieter and less confident.
Bind us together within the fellowship of your Holy
     Spirit
that we may bear one another's burdens
and share one another's joys,
and so fulfil the law of Christ. Amen

Nigel Collinson

114. Teach us, Lord, to bear one another's burdens; and in bearing our own learn when to cast them upon you. At all times enable us to 'rejoice with those who rejoice and weep with those who weep'; for Jesus' sake. Amen

Laurie Campbell

115.   Loving God, our Father and our Mother,
       you call each of us, by name,
       into a community
       in which your love is known and shared.
       Increase our joy in coming together,
       **and transform us into the community
       of your vision.**

       In Christ you brought the weakest
       and smallest into the centre
       and gave them places of honour.
       You showed us how to meet
       around the same table, serving one another,
       washing one another's feet.
       Increase our joy in coming together,
       **and transform us into the community
       of your vision.**

       In Christ you showed us that we are loved
       and accepted in our brokenness.
       You taught us that community is built –
       not only when the weak and poor
       receive from the strong –
       but when the strong learn from the weak,
       the rich from the poor,
       adults from the insights of children . . .
       Increase our joy in coming together,
       **and transform us into the community
       of your vision.**

       Maureen Edwards

116.   Our Father, who makes all humanity one through the
       Holy Spirit, nurture us with your sustaining grace, that
       through fellowship and service we may build each other
       up.   Grant us visions of your Kingdom, and may our
       Church be guided by you, so that all humanity may
       rejoice in your salvation. Amen

       J Emmette Weir, Caribbean

117. Secure in Christ's love we are free to dream:
    of churches being places of fellowship
where no one is ignored or neglected;
    of older people moving heaven and earth
to accommodate today's youth culture;
    of young people experiencing the thrill
of serving with older people;
    of structures initiating and supporting movement
rather than hindering it;
    of our worship being a foretaste of heaven;
of the Holy Spirit empowering ordinary people
    to do undreamed-of things.

Kenneth Todd, Ireland

118. Loving God, Father of children of all ages,
hear the prayer of those who are old in years
but who want to be useful.
Remind us that there is no limit to ways we can serve
    you,
and that we still have minds and hands
to offer in prayer and love to you and to our neighbours.
Help us to give encouragement through a listening ear
and a friendly smile.
In your love, use us still, through Jesus Christ our Lord.

Barbara Eddy

119. Spirit of life, quicken us;
Spirit of power, renew us;
Spirit of truth, inspire us;
Spirit of holiness, purify us;
Spirit of love, make us whole.

Ermal Kirby

120. **Young people**
     Ancient of days and young as each day,
     help us to create a world where dreams come true,
          and the young rise up with new strength.
     We pray for our work with young people
     and for volunteers and youth workers who give time
     in uniformed groups, clubs and fellowships;
     for young people in Seed Teams,
     for those on Time for God Schemes,
     and for the work of MAYC.
     We pray for young people who long for change;
     for the Church
     that must let go of the 'manna' of yesterday
     to feast on the bread of today.
     Instil in us all a youthful longing for the Christ
     who makes 'all things new'.

                                        Mark Wakelin

121. Lord, as you have gathered children into your arms
     and blessed them, so may we open our arms
     to all who are young. May we learn from them,
     walk with them and glimpse your Kingdom within them.

                                        Edward Lacy

122. Holy and loving God,
     root and hold us in your love;
     challenge us with a renewed vision
     of Christ's mission in our world;
     and empower us through the Spirit
     to live as your people
     with love and courage,
     with grace and goodness,
     now and always. Amen

                                        Robin Hutt

123. **Ministers**
Gracious God,
we thank you for the ministers by whom we have been led,
guided and inspired throughout our Christian pilgrimage;
for their dedication, example, preaching and leadership;
for their encouragement and pastoral care,
    particularly in times of special need.
Help us to remember that they are but human, too,
and so to cherish and pray for them,
support and befriend them,
and be sensitive to their needs;
to laugh with them and cry with them
and share gladly in their ministry;
that, together, we may build up the fellowship
of your Church and make it an effective instrument
for mission and service. In Christ's name. Amen

Derek Lyons

124. You speak to us –
in the need of another, in the care of a friend,
in the quiet of the hills and the bustle of the city,
through your word, read or spoken,
in the bread and the wine.
However you speak to us, Lord, help us to respond,
glad of your welcome, eager to obey. Amen

Kenneth Hext

125. May we become a church without walls
open to receive from, and relate to,
the surrounding community,
believing that if the wind of your Spirit
blows through, we will be changed
but not destroyed. Amen

World Village

126.   May your touch on my life, Lord Jesus,
        be as a vine to a branch – a constant communication.
        Nudge me forward when there is opportunity for witness.
        Hold me back when I needlessly rush about.
        Turn me in the right direction when I go wrong.
        Silence my voice when I hog the conversation.
        Embrace me in the arms of your mercy.
        And when my life touches another,
        may it always be in love.
        May my touch on your life, Lord Jesus,
        be as a branch to a vine – a constant communication.

Peter Good, Ireland

127.   **Local preachers**
        Jesus the Carpenter, we pray for those you have called
        from different backgrounds of work and leisure
        to preach your Word.
        May their message, given by your Spirit
        and forged in daily experience,
        be relevant, vital and inspiring
        to all who hear, see and know them.
        Encouraging Lord,
        we pray for all who are testing their call to preach
        and for those with years of experience and service,
        that together they may find inspiration,
        fellowship and mutual support; and that they may grow
            in faith
        as they proclaim the good news of Jesus Christ.
        Risen Lord, when commitment and inspiration burn low,
        deepen their awareness of your living presence
        that brings the life, newness and joy
        to be proclaimed in your name
        and through the power of the Holy Spirit. Amen

Edward Pender

128. Light of the world, enlighten our darkness. Grant your Church courage and humility to be light and salt. In the name of Jesus we offer our prayer. Amen

Zimbabwe

129. As we greet each other in faith:
let our trust in one another mirror your trust in us.

As we greet each other in hope:
let us face the future together with anticipation.

As we greet each other in love:
let our hearts be open to your people,
that the gifts of the Spirit may not be constrained
by fear or culture,
by parochialism or prejudice,
by race or pride,
but might spread through your Church to all the world.

Andrew Pratt

130. Living God,
thank you for the privilege
of belonging to the World Church.
Help us to be open to receive new insights
and so experience renewal
through the worship and spiritual riches
that others have to share with us.
Enable us to understand
what it means to be a pilgrim people
who travel on as part of the worldwide family of God,
united in your way and time
by the grace and the power of Jesus. Amen

Winston Graham, Ireland

131. O God of past, present and future,
in the challenge and excitement of the new,
help us to be grateful for the past.
May we have the grace to be open
to what is different in a fast-changing world,
to allow our faith to be stretched,
as we explore new ways of worship
while retaining the richness of what we already know.
As we give thanks for the wonder
of easy communication with those who are far away,
enable us always to be aware
of people nearby who need our help.
May your whole Church experience
the invigoration of the Holy Spirit
who links us to the earliest followers of Christ,
so that we and all who profess the faith
may go forward in hope into what is yet to be,
in the name of Jesus who shows us the Father,
and who is always with us
in the power of the Holy Spirit. Amen

Thomas Kingston, Ireland

132. We pray for wisdom to discern those traditions which are
still relevant and valuable, and for strength to let go of
those which hinder the gospel for the 21st century, in the
name of Jesus our Contemporary.

Margaret Day

133. Deliver us, O Lord,
from the cowardice that dares not face new truth;
from laziness that is content with half-truth,
and from the arrogance that thinks it knows all truth;
for the sake of Christ our Lord. Amen

Kenya

134.   Earth-quaking God,
        shake the fixtures that have become our prisons.
    Lord of the hurricane,
        sweep the cobwebs entangling us.
    Fiery Spirit,
        refine the impurity of our lives and relationships.
    Renew the face of the earth.
    Renew its communities with harmony and dignity.
    Renew the Church in mission.
    Let us know the calm of your presence, alert for your
        voice.

John Pritchard (adapted)

135.   O God of Resurrection,
    may each moment in our time together
    be open to your healing possibilities.
    Enflame us with your Spirit
    so that, no matter what our age,
    we may experience the hope of the risen Christ,
    the power of Pentecost,
    and your call to be Easter People at all times. Amen

Student of Kgolagano College, Botswana

136.   Heavenly Parent, sharer of humanity,
    Holy Comforter, creating, recreating;
    Your work is going on. It cannot be cut back.
    Thanks for each lesson we learn;
    Thanks for new opportunities;
    Thanks that we can start again:
    We pray in Christ's name. Amen

Otto Wade, Caribbean

137.   God of celebration and daily bread,
       you see us gather in our Sunday best,
       and scatter to farm, office, school and backyard;
       you hear us singing hymns and calypsos,
       sharing gossip and good news;
       you remember the past, with the old,
       and wonder about the future, with the young.
       You touch the world with our hands –
       often hard at work, sometimes forced to be idle.
       Use our hands, our skills,
       our energy, our generosity,
       and build your Church through our lives. Amen

Jan Sutch Pickard

138.   Rainbow God, you have created people of many different
       skin colours, and given us different cultures. But in you
       each has its source and its fulfilment.
       In Jesus Christ you have made us one, breaking down the
       walls that we erect to protect ourselves.
       By your Holy Spirit you have joined us together in one
       body, giving to each part its special gift.
       We pray that in the Church we may experience, more and
       more, the love of your Holy Spirit, a love which honours
       and respects each one, which is sensitive to our hurts and
       hopes, which values the gifts we bring, and shares its
       own treasures with us.
       And to you, O God, Father, Son and Holy Spirit, be all
       honour and glory, now and to ages of ages. Amen

Australian Aboriginal woman

139.   May God raise up more workers after his own heart and
       revive the Church. May he waken our sleepy souls! We
       sometimes pray with tears.

Prayer from China

140.   Blessed Trinity,
        God of Jubilee,
        we turn to you for the life of the Churches.
        Where there is generosity found in us,
            expand it with your grace;
        where our longing for newness has run dry,
            refresh it with your truth;
        where there is creativity of heart,
            deepen it with your wisdom;
        where there is hope of reconciliation,
            add your power to make us one.
        Raise up in us honesty of mind,
            passion for justice,
            and courage to choose your prophetic way.

        Turn your face to us in grace, O God,
        and breathe into us the life of your Spirit.

                                    World Council of Churches

141.   **World Church in Britain Partnership**
        Loving God, we give you thanks
        for the presence and fellowship
        of all who have come from partner Churches
        to serve with us in Britain and Ireland.
        May the gospel insights they share,
        and the gifts they bring,
        enrich the life of our Churches,
        and enable us to enter more fully into what it means
        to be part of your worldwide family.
        Bless all who share with us in this partnership
        and guide us all in a time of change.

                                    Jan Deakin

142.   Before the cross we gather, God of mercy.
       Before the cross we your children gather,
       as the broken body of Christ.

       We turn to you again, seeking healing for division,
       looking back to Jesus who leads us in faith, in love,
           in unity.
       Bring us back, God of grace, smile on us;
       forgive us when we shatter our inheritance
           and go our separate ways.

       As we look to him who endured the cross,
       as we follow him in repentance and waiting,
       we ask you, self-giving God:
       turn us to you and towards each other,
       until we are one as you are One,
       blessed Trinity, now and forever. Amen

                                     World Council of Churches

143.   Loving God, who in Jesus taught the disciples
       to pray and live lives of love,
       so work among us who are slow to learn
       that the same love –
       in which all your laws are fulfilled –
       may be the hallmark of our lives.

                                           Geoffrey Clark

2. Healing

144.   Healer of the nations,
      you welcome all peoples,
      for you are gentle and humble of heart.
      Speak clearly to us: 'Come unto me, all you that are
      weary and are carrying heavy burdens, and I will give
      you rest' *(Matthew 11:28).*
      Sun of righteousness,
      arise with healing in your wings *(Malachi 4:2).*

      True vine,
      we are the branches;
      abide in us as we abide in you,
      so that we may bear much fruit.
      Speak clearly to us: 'Love one another as I have loved
      you' *(John 15:1,4,12).*
      Sun of righteousness,
      arise with healing in your wings.

      Tree of life,
      you give a garland instead of ashes
      the oil of gladness instead of mourning *(Isaiah 61:3).*
      Speak clearly to us: 'For as the earth brings forth its
      shoots, and as a garden causes what is sown in it to spring
      up, so the Lord will cause righteousness and praise to
      spring up before all the nations' *(Isaiah 61:11).*
      Sun of righteousness,
      arise with healing in your wings. Amen

World Council of Churches

145. **Touching place**
O God who comes to meet us
in the secret garden
of our heart:
you walk with us
on awesome and mysterious paths
of great beauty and lasting joy,
and you stay with us
in dangerous and shadowed places
of deep darkness
and searing pain.

When we are touched and held
grant us the wisdom of your Spirit
to meet and recognise you
in one another.

Then take us by the hand
and lead us in the way
of healing love.
Through Jesus Christ we pray. Amen

William C Denning

146. Dear God, through the sensitivity of my ears,
the discernment of my eyes, the clarity of my voice,
bring joy and peace.
Through the lifting of my hands,
the comfort of my arms, the journeying of my feet,
bring joy and peace.
Through the firmness of my faith,
the brightness of my hope, the genuineness of my love,
bring joy and peace:
through Jesus Christ, our Lord. Amen

Ron Hoar

147. Caring and constant God,
you know how our hearts ache –
you have been there too.

Like a mother nursing a sick child on her knee,
like a father who has not given up on his runaway son,
like a friend who is there for someone
who would otherwise die alone,
like a partner coping with a crisis,
or patiently working through a time of change –
you know how our hearts ache –
you have been there too.

When we feel most alone,
when it seems as though everyone has deserted us;
when it would be much easier to give up
and deny the vision;
when we take a step in faith
that is in fact a leap in the dark;
when we face death,
and when we struggle to begin again:
you know how our hearts ache –
you have been there too.

We take courage from your love which has no limits,
your compassion which never fails –
they are new every morning:
caring and constant God.

Jan Sutch Pickard

148. O Blessed Jesus, immortal and victorious, by the sorrow
you suffered when all the powers of your heart failed
you, have mercy on us and help us in our days of
darkness and in our hours of weakness, that we do not
lose hold of you either in this life, or in the life of the
world to come. This we ask for your own name's sake.
Amen

St Bridget of Sweden (1303-73)

149. God of life, when our lives have no music in them, when our hearts are lonely and our souls have lost their courage; flood the path with light, turn our hearts to skies full of promise and quicken our spirits with the memory of your heroes and saints; through Christ our Lord. Amen

St Augustine of Hippo 354-430

150. **In our isolation**
As infants, so recently from the womb, we cry and with our mother's touch are calmed and made secure,
In our isolation, Lord, we cry to you!
As children, shaken by the pain of a fall, seeking solace in a parent's arms,
In our isolation, Lord, we cry to you!
As confused adolescents, enduring the pain of transition from child to adult,
In our isolation, Lord, we cry to you!
As adults in a hostile world seeking others to share our personal island,
In our isolation, Lord, we cry to you!
As age leads to loss of those whose touch we have valued,
In our isolation, Lord, we cry to you!
(Pause)
Your healing touch we recognise in the touch of others, but in our lonely times, when no human touch is near and the fears of life beset us, hold us in your love as
In our isolation, Lord, we cry to you!

Peter Fox

151. May the presence of Christ be seen in his people –
bringing peace to the confused
and friendship to the lonely.
May his love give us courage to be his presence
in the world.

Ian White

152. **Bereavement**
'They have taken *him/her* away and I do not know . . .'
This time last week, last year . . . we were together,
sharing everything, talking, planning for the future . . .
Suddenly the interwovenness of our lives
was broken. So much left unsaid . . .
Only the empty place, and the pain of loneliness.
  S/he is out of reach, beyond touch . . .
  I do not know what that other life is like . . .
  Does *s/he* know what I am going through . . ?
  There is only silence . . .
  No clear answers, no easy way . . .

Come, Lord Jesus Christ, as you came to Mary.
Remind me that what was good about the past
is indestructible; it is part of the joy of heaven.
Take away the paralysis of grief.
Give strength to 'let go' . . .
to 'go and tell' with a deeper compassion
to share the pain of others
and a new understanding of my own vulnerability;
and let me hear again your words of love:
'I will never leave you nor forsake you.'

Maureen Edwards

153. We remember, Lord, the slenderness of the thread which
separates life from death, and the suddenness with which
it can be broken. Help us also to remember that on both
sides of that division we are surrounded by your love.

Persuade our hearts that when our dear ones die neither
we nor they are parted from you.

In you may we find peace, and in you be united with
them in the body of Christ, who has burst the bonds of
death and is alive for evermore, our Saviour and theirs for
ever and ever.

Dick Williams (SPCK)

154. **The death of a baby**
God of small eyes,
Never to open, never to look upon a new day,
Never to see our tears;
God of small hands,
Never to touch nor reach out,
Never to be placed in ours;
God of small, fragile arms,
Never to be held aloft in joy,
Never to hold;
God of small feet,
Never to run, nor even to take a first faltering step;
God of small, shallow breaths,
Never to have voice, to become song,
Never to be laughter;
God of small lives,
Now here, now gone;
God of small, stolen dreams,
Be our comfort.

Elizabeth and Mark Lakin

155. Give me for joy, O Christ, the drying of another's tears;
give me for light, the sunshine of healing their sorrows;
give me for shelter, the shadow of your cross
and for my heart's content, the glory of your presence.
Amen

G A Studdert Kennedy (1883-1929)

156.   *'While love is making all things new'*
      Lord,
      in love, you were in the fertile seed of our beginning
         and in the communion of our conception;
      in love, you were in our eager growth in the womb,
         and you were present at the rawness of our birth;
      in love, you were in the dependency of our childhood,
         and when we broke free to be ourselves;
      in love, you are there in our daily joys and sorrows,
         our triumphs and our failures,
         and in the warmth and cold of daily experience;
      in love you will be there when the wounds of life
         sap our strength and bring the darkness of death.
      Lord of love, of life, of healing, of all-knowing,
         quieten the anxiety of our isolation
         with the experience of your presence
         through which all things are made new
         and united in your purpose.

Peter Fox

157.   Lead us, O Lord,
      from the night of doubt and despair
      into the daylight of dialogue and hope.
      Lead us out of the tomb of suspicion and fear,
      into the life of faith and trust.
      Lead us out of the darkness of terror and hate
      into the sunlight of security and love;
      and lead us out of the gloom of isolation and hurt
      into the healing presence of your glory;
      through Jesus Christ our Lord. Amen

Norman Wallwork

158. **UBUNTU: A prayer for humanness**
Loving God, who in Jesus
willingly took on human form,
come to us again in the flesh,
so that in your humanity
we may recognise the humanity of others.
In these days, when so many feel rejected
        because they are HIV or have AIDS,
speak to us and assure us of your presence
so that we may be there for all who call on us.
Lord, who dares to call us your friends,
touch us with the hands of friendship
so that we may reach out to those who feel untouchable.
Touch us with that second touch of
healing and wholeness of sight
so that we may see others as you see them
and offer your healing power to these
your sisters and brothers.
Spirit of love and life,
breathe into us your compassion and care
so that we may reach out in this place to touch
and to share your love with all.

Daphne and Demetris Palos, South Africa

159. Eternal God,
in Christ your Son, you have touched our lives
with faith and hope and love.
Inspire us by your Spirit, so to touch the lives of others
    with gospel grace
that faith may grow, hope may blossom and love abound;
through Christ our Lord.

Michael Townsend

160. Jesus, you are the Christ who is the Tree of Life.
Your leaves are for the healing of all people.
Grant us this day to shelter in your shade,
that we may clearly see the things which lead
   to health and healing,
      well-being and peace.
Grant us to eat of your fruit,
that we may be strong to work for the health
   of our communities.
Grant us the use of your branches, that we may shelter
   the homeless, defend the weak
and discover creative work for unemployed hands.
Grant us the sweet perfume of your flower,
that in all our efforts we may never lose the wonder
and delight of your presence.

David Moore

161. Liberating Lord,
set your Church free
from structures, status, respectability
to be a voice of prophecy,
to be a hand of healing
and to stand with you
among the homeless, needy and powerless. Amen

World Village

162. Loving God, breathe your Spirit of healing into us,
for we are like clay jars, easily broken, shattered
by the fragility of life and relationships in which you
   place us,
and may your healing grace flow through us into others.
Deepen our awareness of our own need
that we may recognise when others are broken
and be able to share their emptiness and darkness.
In the name of Christ who brings healing. Amen

Maureen Edwards

163. As we remember the love of Jesus
    for all who were sick in body, mind and spirit,
even when they saw only their own need –
we pray for all those who care for the sick:
doctors and nurses,
psychiatrists and physiotherapists,
receptionists and care assistants,
    especially those under great pressure.
Renew their vision of the healing love of Jesus,
and keep them as they work for health and wholeness.
May the vision of your love capture anew our lives
and the lives of all for whom we pray.

May the Spirit of Jesus draw us anew
    to trust and love you,
liberating us from self-concern to love and serve others.

Peter Stephens

164. O Lord Jesus Christ,
on the cross you shed your most precious blood
to bring peace with God;
and by your resurrection you revitalise us with new hope
that 'love is stronger than hate,
good is stronger than evil,
and truth is stronger than falsehood'.
Come to your world today by your life-giving Spirit.
Come, heal the sick and restore the broken.
Come, release the fearful, renew the weak with grace
and save us all for your glory. Amen

Ken Todd, Ireland

165. Hand in hand, united in our risen Lord, let us go forth together, to reach out and touch with love a world in need of healing and peace.
And may the blessing of God, Creator, Saviour, and Enabler, be with us all. Amen

Disley Methodist Church

3. Pilgrimage

166. Loving God, you have called us to set out on our pilgrimage in faith. Help us to travel on with you in hope, sharing your love with all those whom we meet, until together we come to the place where you wait to welcome all your beloved children; through the One who is our Way, Jesus Christ our Lord. Amen

Susan Howdle

167. Grant to us, O Lord, light adequate for each stage of our journey, companions enough to brighten our way and grace sufficient for our pilgrimage through time into eternity; through Christ our Lord. Amen

Norman Wallwork

168. God, our companion,
    walk with us on our pilgrimage of faith,
    and by your presence may our journey
    become more joyful
    as others are encouraged
    to walk in faith with us and with you.

Peter Whittaker

169. May the wisdom of God instruct us; may the hand of God protect us; may the way of God direct us; may the shield of God defend us and may the hosts of God guard us.

St Patrick (c.389-461)

170. Be to us, O Lord, a strong tower of defence; a comforter in every tribulation; and a deliverer in times of distress. In all our troubles be to us a present help, and guide us through all dangers and temptations, till we come at length to the glory and habitation of heaven; this we ask through Jesus Christ our Lord. Amen

Thomas à Kempis (1380-1471)

171. Lord, you are my leader, I have all I need,
you calm me down when I am moody,
you give me energy and love.
You lead me down the right path, even if I'm scared or
    upset.
I will not be afraid, because you are with me and will
    protect me.
You have given me more than I deserve.
I know you will always be there
and your house will be my home for evermore. Amen

Clare Hardwicke

172. God of truth and grace,
by taking the risk of coming among us,
you showed us that you trust us
to care for this wonderful planet and for each other.
Open our eyes and ears to your anger and grief;
help us to trust you and to take the risk
of travelling vulnerably into the unknown,
to do your work joyfully
in the love of our risen Saviour, Jesus Christ. Amen

Mary Ann Ebert

173. We are held in the hollow of God's hand, loved children of the universe, born from the life which flows from God, freed to the fullness of God's creation with all its beauty and variety.

We are all worth dying for in Christ Jesus, all called to the risen life in Christ's resurrection. The way of Jesus gives us footprints to follow, and all our trials and longings are known in the frailty of Christ's birth and the courage of his walking among us.

We are called to new things in the Spirit, in the hope that stirs in unlikely moments, the home we find in the wastelands of our wanderings, the warmth that we touch in the coldness of our need and the opening of our hearts to adventures in belonging.

Caribbean Conference of Churches

174. Gracious Father, we rejoice to know
that your grasp of us is firmer than our hold on you;
remember us when we forget you;
guide us in our wanderings;
come to us when we feel alone
and strengthen us by your Spirit,
in the name of Jesus. Amen

David Reddish

175. Lord, as we face new opportunities,
through the ups and downs which lie ahead,
give us your grace which is always sufficient.
In times of difficulty and despair,
help us to hold on to you;
in times of joy and delight,
help us remember to give thanks.
Day by day, may we deepen our dependence upon you.

Jane Cullen

176. Loving God,
     may we see your presence
     in the tears and laughter of our lives;
     in our wilderness experience may we find hope;
     in the faces of others may we discern your beauty;
     and in our abandonment may we be found by you.
     In Jesus Christ we pray. Amen

Stuart Burgess

177. Creator God, according to your mighty promises
     strengthen us in our weakness, grant us light for your
     path, grace for our trials and help from your holy place;
     through Christ our Lord. Amen

Pakistan

178. Lord, in the wilderness we all hunger after something. It
     may be for justice or freedom or simply to be heard. It
     may be for a smile or compassion or to be loved. You
     are here in the wilderness, and your voice, often like a
     murmur says – My word is sufficient for you, this word
     feeds you. Today, again in the wilderness, having left
     my home country, my family, my friends, I hear your
     voice and your voice feeds me. Having my fill, I will go
     on my way, becoming for the people around no longer a
     wasteland but a haven of restoration. This is my prayer,
     Lord. Amen

Josianne Bidaux, Bhutan

179. God of history and new beginnings,
     Christ of the desert and the sea,
     Spirit of end times and eternity,
         remain with us your people,
         here, now, and wherever we may be.

Ireneu Cunha, Portugal

180. **God with us**
    O God, who travels with us,
        you know who we are.
    We long for life which is full and free.
        We want to move forward in faith
        but the way seems so dangerous;
    we stand in helpless fear
    before the hiddenness in our past
        and in our future. *Silence*
    Stand beside us, gentle Christ:
    Walk before us, brave Jesus.
    Call us on into life, Holy Spirit.

    Hear the word to us in Christ:
    I will never leave you nor forsake you,
        even to the end of time.
    I will walk with you down the pathways of death
    and lead you to eternal life. Amen

    World Council of Churches

181. You are my refuge and strength.
    When my foot slips, your mercy, O God, supports me
    and your comfort makes my soul rejoice.
    You supply all my needs
    and sustain me with my daily bread . . .
    With you, I live a life of abundance
    as you have promised me.
    How great and marvellous are your works!

    Hna. Elvia Aviles, Panama

182. Loving and holy God, you share all our journeying
    and wait ahead of us wherever we go:
    in times of light, may we walk in joyful gratitude;
    in times of darkness, may we walk with faithful courage;
    and as we travel into the unknown,
        may we walk in certain hope.

    Robin Hutt

183. Let us be glad, O Lord, to receive from your hand a reflection of the seasons in our souls; the clarity and cleansing of the winter frost, the refreshment and brightness of the spring, the healing and burning heat of the summer and the peace and gentleness of the autumn shadows; and with all else the gift of yourself; through Christ our Lord. Amen

Jane de Chantal (1572-1641)

184. Lord of the years,
help us to recognise and respond
to your love in every season of our life:
the spring of childhood,
the summer of youth and adulthood,
the autumn of our maturity
and the winter of our age.
We rejoice in your grace sufficient for each day.
We praise you for the past
and trust you for the future. Amen

David Reddish

185. Holy God,
beneath the deepest peace
and most turbulent strife
you hold all things together,
and in Jesus you show us your love
that nothing can break.
Help us in our calm certainties
and in our disturbing questions
to rest in your strength,
to be fed by your Spirit,
and to trust in Christ's way,
that in all seasons of life we may walk with you,
through Jesus Christ our Lord. Amen

Robin Hutt

186. Lord, when I walk in the darkness be my light; when I am lonely be my companion; when I am weak come to my help; when I am restless grant me your peace and when I am bitter fill me with your patience and love; for Jesus' sake. Amen

Dietrich Bonhoeffer (1906-45)

187. Support us, O Lord, all the day long, until the shades lengthen, and the evening comes, the busy world is hushed, the fever of life is over, and our work done. Then, Lord, in your mercy grant us a safe lodging, a holy rest and peace at the last; through Jesus Christ our Lord. Amen

John Henry Newman (1801-90)

188. We are wayfarers, following roads to the ends of the earth,
pilgrims on our way to the end of the age.
Behold, I am with you to the end of the age.
We are travellers on the road to freedom,
a community of grace with good news for all we meet.
Behold, I am with you to the end of the age.
We'll travel lightly, travel together, learn as we go;
we are disciples, our mission is love, the journey is long.
Behold, I am with you to the end of the age.
We travel with authority, fearful of none;
we are sent, opponents of evil, heralds of hope.
Behold, I am with you to the end of the age.
We travel with humility, no task is too small;
we are servants, the cross is our compass, love is our sign.
Behold, I am with you to the end of the age.
When the way is uncertain, shadows are sinister,
and dangers threaten,
we'll not be afraid, but take heart.
Behold, I am with you to the end of the age.

The Philippines

189. Living God,
      when we feel the shaking of the foundations
      and try to retreat into the security of the past,
      teach us that you are the God of the future.

      Living God,
      when we are tempted to despair,
      when events move so quickly
      and it seems that there is no way forward,
      teach us that you are the God of hope.

      Living God,
      when things happen beyond our understanding
      and we find our trust in you is threatened,
      teach us that you are the God of all faith.

      Living God,
      in a fast-moving world, when we find our values
          questioned
      and it is not easy to perceive what is right,
      teach us that you are the God of all wisdom.

      So may we learn to live each day
      in company with you
      and to follow you wherever you will lead us. Amen

Nigel Collinson

190. Lord, you persevered in your mission and calling
      despite hostile critics and fickle crowds.
      You moved as a pilgrim
      on the pathway of loving obedience to your Father
      even when friends deserted you.
      Grant us to follow you through thick and thin
      in response to your call, 'Follow me'.

Edward Lacy

191. *Grist ein Gwaredwr, tyrd atom i fyw, fel yr awn ymaith a goleuni dy obaith yn ein llygaid, a'th ffydd a'th gariad yn ein calonnau.*

O Christ our Redeemer, come and dwell with us, so that we may go forward with the light of your hope in our eyes, and your faith in our hearts.

Martin Evans-Jones, Wales

192. O God,
help me to walk in the boots of the miner,
the shoes of the trader,
the moccasins of the trapper,
and in the sandals of Jesus Christ the Master,
and to see others as he would see them.

Canadian Indian

193. Loving God, we know you and see you in Jesus:
so come to us in friendship
and walk with us along the way,
that when the pathway is rocky and uphill
we may know your strength and, in all circumstances,
have eyes which are open to others,
that we may be to them instruments of your purpose,
sharing faith through encouragement and love.

Geoffrey Clark

194. God of encouragement
help us to remember
that the journey of a thousand miles
begins with the first step.

Kenneth Todd, Ireland

195. God our Father, in this house of prayer you bless your family on its earthly pilgrimage: so quicken our consciences by your holiness, nourish our minds by your truth, purify our imaginations by your beauty, and open our hearts to your love, that, in the surrender of our wills to your purpose, the world may be renewed in Jesus Christ our Lord. Amen

William Temple (1881-1944)

196. May all created things praise you, O Lord. May you be blessed in the fellowship of human hearts. May you be worshipped by the exile, hallowed by the pilgrim and adored by the saints; until together we come to the palace of your heavenly glory; and this we ask through Christ our Lord. Amen

St Teresa of Avila (1515-82)

197. Lord, you have brought us near to an innumerable company of angels, and to the spirits of the just made perfect. Grant us, during our earthly pilgrimage, to live in their fellowship, and in our heavenly country to become partakers of their joy. Amen

William Bright (1824-1901)

198. Loving God,
we thank you for all who have died
and especially for those who have inspired us.
Help us to continue the journey
and have courage and hope in time of despair.

Stuart Burgess

199. Lord, we cannot properly reflect on the meaning
      of the cross
  while life is easy and comfortable.
  Let us follow you on your way to Golgotha
  again and again, bearing the pain and sin of humanity,
  yet directing all our deep questions to you, you alone.
  Loving God, you create and recreate;
  you allow all things to die and you bring to life.
  Let us not aspire to glory without suffering,
  confidence without self-denial,
  or eternal life without dying.

  Israel Selvanayagam, Church of South India

200. Lord, we give thanks for those who enrich
      and sustain our lives.
  We give thanks for those who, in their poverty,
      lead us to your love.
  We pray that, in you, we may have hope
      in our frustration, failure and despair.
  In Jesus Christ we pray. Amen

  Stuart Burgess

201. Blessing and honour to God the Father, who is our hope.
  Blessing and honour to God the Son, who is our refuge.
  Blessing and honour to God the Holy Spirit,
      who is our protection.
  Blessing and honour to the Holy Trinity, the one true
      God,
      glorious now and for ever. Amen

  Orthodox Compline, after St Ioannikios, d. 834

4. Strength in weakness

202. Strengthen our weakness with your compassion, O Lord,
and comfort us with your loving kindness. Amidst the
changing fortunes of this world may we find rest in your
peace. May we find cleansing in your presence and the
enlightenment of your Holy Spirit all our days; through
Christ our Lord. Amen

Nestorian Liturgy

203. Let there be no day on which you say,
    'There is no one to help me.'
Let there be no day on which you say,
    'There is no one to walk with me.'
Let there be no day on which you say,
    'There is no hope.'
And may God who encourages us to take the first step
and who gives us the hope of reconciliation,
give us his blessing and flood our hearts
with the joy of life. Amen

Source unknown

204. Only when we are weak, O Lord, are we strong: as we
pass through the vale of suffering grant us the gift of your
safety and peace, the gentleness of your Spirit and a sense
of your mercy and love, through Jesus Christ our Lord.
Amen

Jeremy Taylor (1613-67)

205. Behold, Lord, an empty vessel that needs to be filled.
My Lord, fill it. I am weak in the faith; strengthen me. I
am cold in love; warm me and make me fervent, that my
love may go out to my neighbour. I do not have a strong
and firm faith; at times I doubt and am unable to trust you
altogether. O Lord, help me. Strengthen my faith and
trust in you. Amen

Martin Luther (1483-1546)

206. Guide us, O Lord, in all the changes of this uncertain
world, that we may live in your peace. Let us not
complain in our troubles, nor grow proud in our
prosperity. With calmness of faith, let us rejoice in the
goodness of your perfect will; through Christ our Lord.
Amen

Jeremy Taylor (1613-67)

207. Give to me, O God, a heart of joy that rests in your peace
and a soul of tranquillity that delights in your beauty; a
spirit of glory that sings your praise, a life of serenity at
home in your presence and a mind of quietness renewed
by your Spirit; through Jesus Christ our Lord. Amen

Evelyn Underhill (1875-1941)

208. Father, Creator of this warm and rainwashed Celtic land,
we feel your power in the majesty of towering cliff
and restless sea;
in wooded creek and sandy cove,
adorned with flowers and teeming with wildlife.
Recharge us with the power of your Spirit,
which surges with sacrificial love for others,
that conflict and pain may be burnt up
in hope and harmony
as we follow the path of our Living Lord. Amen

Daphne Train

209. Stay with us, O Lord, when we are swamped by weariness and seeming impossibilities. Turn our faces gently towards you, keep our hearts loving and our will determined to fight on to the end.

Mother Janet Stuart (1857-1914)

210. O God, in mystery and silence you are present in our lives, bringing new life out of destruction, hope out of despair and growth out of difficulty. We thank you that you do not leave us alone, but are working with us to bring new things to birth. Help us to perceive your hand in the unfolding of our lives, to know the dignity of acceptance within your family and to work to make all human life full of purpose and joy. Amen

Kathleen Richardson

211. Lord of life,
    when the rhythm of my life
    is disturbed by fear or sorrow,
    when harmony is jarred by discord,
    when I am out of tune with you and the world –
    help me to sing a new song
    of faith and hope,
    peace and love,
    joy and praise. Amen

Gwen Charlton

212. May the calm of our Lord's presence
        still the storms of our stress;
    may the coolness of his touch
        assuage our anxieties;
    may the clarity of his vision
        clear our confusion;
    and may he give us courage to claim his peace.

Rosemary Watters

213. Let not faith fall my sister,
Let not hope fall my brother,
When times are hard,
When tiredness comes,
Trust in the Lord my sister.

Rejoice and receive the risen Christ,
The gifts of grace, peace and life . . .

Bolivia

214. Lord Jesus Christ, we hold up our weakness to your strength;
our failure to your faithfulness; our sinfulness to your perfection. Cleanse us by your Holy Spirit and hide us in the wounds of your love; now and forever. Amen

Mother Janet Stuart (1857-1914)

215. Almighty God, you hold us when we feel insecure,
lift us when we stumble
and make us strong enough to go on when the going is
hard.
We thank you for your startling love and intervening
care,
turning our weakness into strength
and our hesitating efforts into useful service.

Geoffrey Clark

216. Dear Lord, when your way is hard to find,
guide my next step;
when your truth is hard to know,
inform my next decision;
when life is hard to bear,
help me through this day. Amen

Thomas McKnight, USA/Ireland

217. We greet you, Spirit of the North.
      You are the cold, biting wind that blows across our land,
      that strips the earth of all that is dead and decayed,
      that robs us of the false securities, so easily blown away.
      Teach us to plant our feet securely on the earth
      and to see things as they really are,
      that the coming of your Spirit may find us standing firm
          in integrity.
      It is your Spirit whose winds bring the snow of winter,
      with their fury and their solitude.
      It is your Spirit who blankets the earth for sleep.
      Teach us, Spirit of the North, in the solitude of winter,
      to wait in darkness with the sleeping earth,
      believing that we, like the earth,
      already hold within ourselves the seeds of new life.

Canadian Indian

218. Gracious God, you seek us at every moment of our lives.
      When the sun is shining it is not too difficult
      to believe in you and to live thankfully.
      But the hardest times are when our minds
      are filled with anxiety and dread,
      or when we are tired out with caring for others.
      Give us then the wings of your Spirit,
      not to escape from all that we must do,
      but to face it with a calm mind,
      aware of your unfailing presence.

Nigel Collinson

219. Father, O mighty force,
      That force which is in everything,
      Come down between us, fill us,
      Until we are like you.

West African Traditional

220. Grant to us, O Lord, the royalty of inward happiness and the serenity which comes from living close to you. Daily renew in us the sense of joy and fill our whole life with your light and grace . . . and in all things let us give thanks to the God and Father of our Lord Jesus Christ. Amen

Robert Louis Stevenson (1850-94)

221. Loving God,
whose love enfolds us on the lowest of days
and gives us new hope when our candle burns low,
set us alight with that same love
that we may share the presence of Jesus day by day.
Amen

Geoffrey Clark

222. Lord, may nothing perturb us and nothing make us frightened; for all things are passing and you alone are changeless. Those who possess you lack nothing and you alone meet all our needs. Amen

St Teresa of Avila (1515-82)

223. O God of love, grace and truth,
We give you thanks for family and friends,
for hope in times of despair,
for light in times of darkness,
for showing us the way to life,
for strength to endure to the end,
and for your love and the blessings we cannot count.

Lesley G Anderson, Panama

III

Our Calling – Being a good neighbour

1. Building community

224.   Wondrous and holy God, Creator of the universe,
you make all people in your own image,
you live and work in our midst.
You bless us with an immense variety of cultures
and ways of responding to you.
You show us new patterns of living and loving in Jesus.
You give us strength by your Holy Spirit.
We bless and thank you.

Forgive all among us
who put boundaries around your presence, love and
    work;
who use diversity to divide people –
to demonise some and accord privileged status to others;
who seek to dominate or destroy those who are different.
Have mercy on us all.

Show us all how to live and work with others;
to receive diversity as a gift and not as a threat;
to move beyond tolerance of those who are different
to mutual respect and trust.
Show us the art of listening with respect to one another.
Grant us the help of your Spirit
that, in humility, we may share with others
our faith and story.
In the name of Christ. Amen

Inderjit Bhogal

225. Lord God, make the door of my house wide enough to receive all who need love and fellowship and narrow enough to shut out all envy, pride and hate. May its threshold be smooth enough to put no stumbling block in the way of your lost or little ones; and may it be rugged enough to foil the tempter's power. May the entrance to my home be for some the gateway to your eternal Kingdom, through Christ our Lord.

Thomas Ken (1631-1711)

226. Father of all humankind,
make the roof of my house wide enough for all opinions,
oil the door of my house so it opens easily to friend and
stranger,
and set such a table in my house
that my whole family may speak kindly and freely
around it.

Hawaii

227. Come, God of the city, into my city.
Put up a sign, 'Danger – God at work'.
Build places of welcome . . . places to play –
riotous sound and colour;
Build homes of celebration with friend and stranger;
Build places of worship . . . places to pray –
spaces to listen and rest in quietness;
Illuminate with your energy,
Add your wine to my parties,
Your generosity to my economy,
And offer hospitality through my openness. Amen

Janet Corlett

228. Lord, help us to take good care of the paths between the houses, to use them to meet each other, for if they are not used they will become overgrown with thistles and even harder to pass. Make us communities of love, strong enough and open enough to include others. Amen

Donald Eadie

229. Triune God, we come before you with our deep longing
          for true community;
      between young and old, between men and women,
      rich and poor, between all races.
      We long to overcome the divisions between Christians.
      Help us to overcome the many barriers we erect.
      Help us to dispel our suspicions
      that we may see the good intentions in those we meet.
      Help us to put aside our uncertainty
      that we may appreciate the dignity of others.
      Help us to cast out our fears
      that we may allay the fears of others.
      Help us to conquer our pride
      that we may love our neighbours as ourselves.
      Grant us the gift of true community in reconciliation
          with others.

European Ecumenical Assembly, Graz

230. Lord Jesus Christ, come to us in the power of the Spirit
      that we may take initiatives in mending broken
          relationships.
      Give us perseverance in breaking down barriers
          of suspicion and mistrust;
      insight to recognise our prejudices;
      courage to admit our failures;
      honesty to acknowledge our festering hurts
      and a willingness to repent of our personal and
          community sins.
      Help us to prove that your grace is sufficient for every
          need.

Ian D Henderson, Ireland

231. Train us, Lord, and send us out to do the impossible,
      because behind the impossible are your grace and
      presence; we cannot fall into the abyss.

Peru

232. O Lord,
  we come in humility
  before your throne of grace
  and thank you for the examples you have left us.
  You gave your love and your time to all people.
  You praised the widow who gave her last coin to the
    Temple;
  you received Nicodemus during the night;
  you called Matthew to the apostolate;
  you visited Zacchaeus in his home;
  you gave yourself to the suffering poor;
  you spent long hours in prayer.
  We hear your voice, 'As the Father has sent me,
  even so I send you' *(John 20:21).*
    Help us to share your mission.

Lesley G Anderson, Panama

233. As we remember the love of Jesus
    for the outcast in society:
  the beggar and the criminal,
  the swindler and the prostitute –
  we pray for all your people,
    especially those who work in deprived areas.
  Renew their vision of the universal love of Jesus,
  and strengthen them in seeking to serve
    the most needy and neglected.
  May the vision of your love capture anew our lives
  and the lives of all for whom we pray.

  May the Spirit of Jesus draw us anew
    to trust and love you,
  liberating us from self-concern to love and serve others.

Peter Stephens

234. Dear God, our Father, we lift our voices to you in community prayer; help us to be faithful to your call.
May we know your will, follow your way, carry out your mission, in love, to all people. Give us strength to take our stand for life against all the forces of death. In the name of Jesus, the Way, the Truth and the Life. Amen

Methodist Church in Brazil

235. Father, guide and protect us at the beginning of a new century. Keep us safe, O Lord. Bring hope to our hearts, so that each of us will see your light to brighten our days as we travel with you.
We pray for those who have died that they may know your peace, because they are with you where no harm can come to them . . .
Father, we live in a troubled world where, at times, it seems that evil has the upper hand. We believe that the time will come when you will say, 'Enough is enough.'
Father, protect our children because you know they are our future; strengthen them as they grow and journey into adulthood. We will continue to put our trust in you.
Father, grant us grace to understand and follow in your footsteps.

Doreen Lawrence

236. Loving God, who has called *ordinary* people
into *extraordinary* work for your Kingdom,
we pray for those facing difficult decisions
and situations, as they forge new links
between sections of the community
across issues of race and faith.
We pray for those working imaginatively
with other Christian people;
and for ourselves as we seek to express
your love for all humanity where we are.
Father, Son and Holy Spirit, make all things new.

Keith Burrow

237. Lord, you would be at home in our District:
      you would enjoy walking in the hills
      and rejoice in the cosmopolitan nature of our major city;
      you would welcome the challenge of our places of
            learning
      and respect the skill of people who work with their
            hands;
      you would stop and listen to those who farm the land,
      and delight in conversations in our village streets.
      You would be amazed by the faith in some of our
            churches.
      Lord, you would feel at home in our District.

      You would be concerned for the unemployed,
      and the numbers of homeless people on our streets;
      you would be angry at the unequal distribution of wealth,
      and saddened to see our local shops forced to close
      by out-of-town shopping centres;
      you would be upset by the funding difficulties of our
            hospitals
      and disturbed by the failure to care in our community.
      You would be distressed by our complacency.
      Lord, you would feel at home in our District.

      We are comforted and challenged,
      encouraged and disturbed because you are at home
            among us.
      Thank you, Lord.

                                          David Halstead

238. God of green and pleasant places
      and of dark uncomfortable situations,
      you call your people to be in every part of your creation.
      Give us courage and wisdom
      to leave behind some of those things
      that are easy to cherish,
      and to walk in love where we are needed most,
      with Jesus Christ. Amen

                                          Alan Anderson

239. God of faithful love, help us to trust you,
as institutions and cultures of which we are a part
change – and threaten our securities.
Inspire with vision, courage and determination
those who lead companies, businesses and organisations.
Empower those who provide services to work
with integrity and to the highest professional standards.

Spirit of Love, renew relationships in all places of work,
and sustain care for customers and clients.
Life-giving Spirit, nourish families and communities
with the costly dedication of neighbours and friends.
Make us bold to share the stresses of everyday work;
help us to listen to the concerns of people about their
     work.
May people discern the power of your gospel
where they work, and praise your name.

David Deeks

240. Lord our God, help us to be peacemakers in our place of
work; and at all times to share the pain and hurt of others;
to offer enthusiasm and joy, to warn the idle, to
encourage the timid and support the weak; through Christ
our Lord. Amen

Laurie Campbell

241. Generous God,
you never cease to pour out your love on all people
in spite of what we do in our selfishness and narrowness.
Strengthen us that we may be generous in our love:
that we may never fail to welcome others,
even if their standards are different from our own;
that we may always respond to the needs of others,
though it may be costly to ourselves;
and that we may have confidence
that our loving will help to change the world;
through Jesus Christ whose death on a cross
     marks the victory of love.

Graham Carter

242. **The workplace**
Christ the carpenter,
who knew the rigours and rewards of a hard day's work,
we pray for all who work for the good of the community,
using physical strength or mental agility,
understanding people or serving their needs,
often doing repetitive and tedious jobs.
You revealed your power in humility and service,
and so we pray for employers, managers and supervisors
that they may be fair, honest and considerate in the
demands they make and the rewards they give.

You showed us how to identify
with the needs of individuals, and so we pray
for all who are unable to find employment.
Grant them strength to cope with frustration,
disappointment and depression;
enable them to maintain hope and self-esteem,
and guide them into the work you need them to do.

Lord, we pray for ourselves in our daily work
that the power of your love may work through us,
that your divine purpose may be fulfilled,
and that all we do may be to your praise and glory.

Ian Preece

243. God, whose Son was a carpenter, we remember before
you all those in our community involved in industry and
commerce;
those who make things, those who plan and prepare
budgets, those who work in industrial relations and those
who make decisions.
Within the complexities of our community life, where
there are many dilemmas and contradictions, may men
and women be strengthened to make good decisions and
to exercise an influence for the values that you have
placed at the heart of all life.

Nigel Collinson

244. **The farming community**
God of the heavens and the earth,
you call us to share in the care of creation
and to bring food and fruitfulness from field and farm.
Hear our prayer for all who make their living on the land
in this time of crisis and anxiety.
We pray for farmers, their families and communities
and all who depend on them.
Lord, in your mercy: **hear our prayer.**

For agricultural chaplains, support groups
and rural churches,
Lord, in your mercy: **hear our prayer.**

For restraint and fairness in the use of economic power,
For discernment and a long view in policy and decision,
For love of creation in farm policy and practice,
For justice in world trade,
Lord, in your mercy: **hear our prayer.**

For ourselves that we may eat with joy and with care,
For land and livestock
and love for those who care for them,
Lord, in your mercy, **hear our prayer.**

Farm Crisis Network

245. God, you are all in all.
Help us as we touch the spade, the soil, the seeds,
To feel you springing up within us.

Malcolm Braddy

246. **Rural life**

We pray for our fragile earth. Yesterday –
wild flowers, streams of clear water, busy farms.
Today – farmers bankrupt, streams polluted, flowers
    gone.
May we value creation, now, and be wise in its use.
God of creation, fertilise our minds.

We pray for the peace of the countryside. Yesterday –
quiet paths and byways.
Today – fast cars in narrow streets, crime in dark lanes.
May we recognise the good, now, despite the darkness.
God of light, clarify our vision.

We pray for a changing community. Yesterday –
its heart the church, the village shop.
Today – the shop closed, the church empty.
May we grow more aware of one another's needs.
God, all-embracing, infuse in us your caring.

We pray for a shrinking world. Yesterday –
divided by size and distance.
Today – Emails, the Internet, telecommunication,
    satellite.
May we, in our insularity, be drawn closer to one
    another.
God of this one world,
bind us to our neighbour, everywhere. Amen

Alice Crosland

247. **The farming community**
We pray for all who work the land, care for livestock and fish the seas. Especially at this time, we pray for members of the farming community who are facing ruin and an uncertain future.
Lord, in your mercy: **hear our prayer.**

We pray for farming families who are isolated physically and socially; for farmers obliged to sell their livestock for a pittance; for those who watch helplessly as old values are threatened and a familiar way of life vanishes; for those whose livelihood depends on the farming industry; for those in the grip of anxiety, fear and depression; for those who must give up the farm and leave the land.
Lord, in your mercy: **hear our prayer.**

We pray for the welfare of animals during these times of financial pressure; for those who work in the Ministry of Agriculture, Fisheries and Food; for all decision-makers in this land and throughout Europe; for agricultural chaplains who meet people at the point of their deepest needs, and offer love and understanding.
Lord, in your mercy: **hear our prayer.**

The Arthur Rank Centre

248. Lord Jesus, all our work is yours,
     all our world is yours.
Grant unto us the joy of forgetting no one and nothing;
the love of caring for all people and everything you have
     made;
the peace of knowing that we are working with you in
     your plan;
     for your Kingdom's sake. Amen

Amos Cresswell

249. **A driver's prayer**
Lord, be beside me at the wheel
Sharpen my mind as I drive through town,
Tired, stressed and eager to reach home.
The day crowds in: conversations, deals . . .
Help me keep focused on the road,
Anticipate the dangers –
Can I stop if the lights turn red?
Will I see that child ahead?
The silent cyclist in the dark,
The van reversing, trying to park,
Car doors opening,
Motorcyclists overtaking,
Black ice, wet leaves.
Let me kill only my speed!
Lord, be beside me at the wheel.

Gill Murray

250. **For our schools**
We thank you, God, for all who work untiringly in our
schools for the benefit of our children. Thank you that,
amid complex challenges so many teachers are
committed to the spiritual, moral and educational needs
of all pupils.
We pray for teachers under pressure, especially when an
OFSTED inspection draws near, or an adverse OFSTED
report has been received; that they may continue to
motivate and inspire children in spite of continued
criticism, league-tables, money constraints, and
increasing problems caused by disruptive pupils and
truancy.
We pray that staff may remain dedicated to all pupils in
their care, motivating, praising and encouraging them;
for head teachers amid the ever-increasing stress and
responsibility they have to handle.
We pray for children who are unhappy at school, and
especially for those who are physically or mentally
bullied.
May we never forget the aim of education to develop the
character and potential of all children, that they may
become worthy citizens and responsible, helpful
members of society.

Geoff Tilzey

251. **We pray for children**
    for children who can run and skip, dance and jump,
        and children who long to run but can only watch;
    for children who laugh and tell jokes,
        and children who cry themselves to sleep;
    for children who have loving, happy homes,
        and children whose homes are torn apart;
    for children who learn to trust because those around
        them are trustworthy,
        and children who have learnt to trust nobody;
    for children who are excited and hopeful,
        and children who have lost all hope.
    We pray for children,
        for *all* our children who teach us about life,
        who look to tomorrow, whatever their today.

Judy Jarvis

252. God of love –
    You said to your disciples, 'Let the children come to
        me.'
    You set a child in the midst and said, 'Be like this.'
    You taught that anyone who welcomes a child welcomes
        you,
    and anyone who harms a child will know your anger.
    Redeem our sins, save those at risk, and bless each one
        of us.

    God of celebration –
    You asked a small boy for his packed lunch,
    and made sure that everyone in the crowd had enough to
        eat –
    and there were still crumbs to feed the birds.
    Help us to receive what children have to give
    in their generosity, their wonder and their laughter.
    God of compassion –
    You took a young girl by the hand, saying:
    'She is not dead, she is asleep . . . Get up my child.'
    Help us to protect all children from the death of
        innocence,
    so that in good time we may all grow,
    in grace, to the people you mean us to be. Amen

Jan Sutch Pickard

253. Loving Creator,
we pray for children who will be born today
to women who are young, to women who are ageing:
children born into poverty,
children born into insecurity,
children born into well-organised households,
children born into difficult circumstances,
children whose coming has been long-awaited,
children whose coming was not anticipated;
children who have been born today,
    defenceless and vulnerable –
    children who are your creation,
    citizens of your Kingdom.

Rosemary Wass

254. **The family**
Loving, creative God,
we thank you that you did not create us to be alone
but set us to live in relationship with other people
    and with you.
Thank you for the people who are important in our lives:
those who have made us what we are
and those whose lives have enriched ours;
for friends and family, and those who bring us joy;
for those for whom we care and those who care for us.

We pray for all who are finding life difficult today:
those who are separated from friends and family;
those whose relationships are oppressive or violent,
    or broken beyond repair;
those whose daily life is a struggle against poverty
    or discrimination.
We pray for all in the world who will die this day
    and for those who will be born;
for those who grieve for loved ones they have lost
and those who will celebrate new life.

David Gamble

255. God of grace,
whose love embraces us,
enable us to reach out to others
so that, through us, your love may be known.
Lord, hear us: *Lord, graciously hear us.*

God of justice,
free us from the confines of culture
that we may be the voice of the voiceless,
the oppressed and the hungry.
Lord, hear us: *Lord, graciously hear us.*

God of hope,
strengthen those who search for a purpose in life;
those whose lives lack quality;
those who have lost their way.
Lord, hear us: *Lord, graciously hear us.*

God of all people,
hasten the day when we may recognise
that your Kingdom is for all your people.
Lord, hear us: *Lord, graciously hear us.*

Drugarog Dduw
tyrd, aros gyda ni.
I'n galw unwaith eto
i gerdded yn dy ffyrdd. Amen

Eluned Williams

256. Lord God of the towel and basin, who washed
the disciples' feet,
give us a growing understanding
of your capacity to love and show mercy;
give us boldness to take up towel and basin
with a deeper sense of compassion to serve our
neighbours;
give us courage to walk the way of the cross.
Jesus the servant, build and nurture your Church,
that we may live to your praise and glory. Amen

Christine Walters

2. People in special need

257. Lord, help us to recognise need in the ordinary routine of
     life,
     encourage us to look beneath the surface,
     unfold to us signs of hardship,
     areas of tension
     and shadows of despair.
     Your touch is needed where people hurt;
     help us to reach out with your loving concern. Amen

Terence Isherwood

258. We give thanks for the beauty, vitality and diversity of
     creation; for Christ seen in the faces of our fellow human
     beings.
     We pray for those living on the edge: the poor and lonely,
     the alienated, the strangers in our midst; those isolated by
     mental or physical illness, by bereavement or family
     breakdown; who have crossed frontiers or missed out on
     education; those who slip through the net of social caring,
     whose voices are unheard, who are not quite respectable
     (though worthy of respect);
     for ourselves, that we may learn from our sisters and
     brothers about resilience and hope against the odds, about
     celebration and sharing, that we may never make
     assumptions, or make the Church exclusive when God's
     love includes all.

Jan Sutch Pickard

259. Praying with older people

Living God, whose love in Christ makes all things new,
we rejoice in the opportunities retirement brings to
　　many;
and, as we recognise the personal losses
　　and failing health which often come with ageing,
we pray for a renewal of inner strength for older people.
Reassure those drawing near
　　to the end of their earthly lives.
Bless the work of Methodist Homes
　　in caring for over 5000 people in residential homes,
　　sheltered housing and Live at Home support.
Help old and young to affirm each other in family,
　　church and community,
　　and so restore a richer health to humankind.

Albert Jewell

260. For those with failing sight

We who can see thank God for the gift of sight. May we
look with joy and understanding at the world around us
and all who share it with us. May we be ready to share
our vision, quite literally, with those who cannot see so
well or not at all.

We who see only dimly thank God for partial sight:

for memory, for imagination and expectation, which can
help to compensate for disability;

for friends who help without fussing, for audio books and
newspapers, for music and the spoken word;

for all gadgets that maximise our involvement in normal
life – from the electronic equipment we use at home to
the simple beep of a pedestrian crossing that lets us cross
the road in safety;

for music and the spoken word, for birdsong, for the
smell of baking bread or new-mown grass; for everything
that reminds us that only one of our senses is on the
blink.

May we have grace to accept reality with humour.

Patricia Smith

261. **The power of touch**
Lord,
In a woman's desperate need for healing
    you experienced the power of touch.
Help us, for whom the power of touch has been darkened
    by abuse, to rediscover its power to heal.
Lift from us the reserve
    which would deny its life-giving strength
    to those isolated by the modern leprosy of AIDS.
Help us to learn from those whose lifestyle is not ours,
    yet whose experience of life and sickness and death
    has opened new avenues to understanding.
Empower us to love, through the power of touch:
    to bring light, not darkness;
    to bring warmth, not the coldness of fear and
        prejudice;
    to bring hope where there is despair;
    to proclaim new life where there is the sadness of
        death.

Peter Fox

262. **The pain of touch**
God, who in creation touches the world,
and through your Son seeks to touch each one of us;
what does your touch mean for women and men
for whom touch is a commercial transaction?
Hate, scorn, possession, power;
yet providing food and shoes for their children?
The disregarded touch of a client;
exploitation, fear, risk, uncertainty.
The sharp touch of the needle;
welcome rush of oblivion.
How does your touch reach those
whom life has taught to protect themselves
from being touched?
May the possibility of the touch of love,
real love and the freedom that love brings,
be known by every one of us.
In the name of Jesus, who touches
and is touched by the life of the world. Amen

Brenda Mosedale

263. **She is only a child**
    She is only a child, Lord!
    A child who carries within her another child.
    Her father had wanted her, had flattered her with warm soft words, had used the guile of experience to achieve his aim, and rationalised his right to her body.
    She is only a child, Lord!
    A child who carries within her another child.
    She had not been used to kindness in his voice. Ever-present anger and crude expletive were her world and to be wanted had seemed good.
    She is only a child, Lord!
    A child who carries within her another child.
    But kindness in a voice without love becomes cool and silent. His desire was short-lived and, with his need for novelty, he had gone, stamping his embargo on the truth with a seal of fear. Locking in her mind for ever the new knowledge.
    She is only a child, Lord!
    A child who carries within her another child.
    Perhaps there had been safety in the anger. Less destruction than that achieved by false kindness with its hidden aim.
    She is only a child, Lord!
    A child who carries within her father's child.
    She is only a child, Lord!
    And for her and all her sisters throughout the world
    at this time of change,
    In silence, we pray that they may know Love *(Silence).*

    Peter Fox

264. **Homelessness**

Being homeless is no JOKE.
You have no sleep,
no privacy, no dignity.
You are treated like a leper.
You have no money.
No hope. You drift from day to day.
You cannot get any relief from fellow vagrants
who only talk to you if you have any money for drink.
The police harass you.
You get no Social Security;
you are always being moved on.
I have had my box stolen, my blankets, shoes.

Paul, a user of the West London Mission Day Centre

We pray for all homeless and rootless people throughout the country as they struggle for dignity and security; for all agencies who seek to reach out and help those at the edges of our society. May we recognise that it is at the margins where good news and grace are most often discovered.

West London Mission

265. **NCH Action for Children**

Eternal God, whose Son was born in a stable,
exiled in childhood,
and who had 'nowhere to lay his head',
we bring to you our prayers
for your children who are homeless today.
Show us where love and compassion are needed;
'where there is darkness, let us bring your light;
where there is despair, let us bring hope.'
Grant that through our action
the homeless and the vulnerable may find refuge
and security. We pray this
in and through the One who showed us his love,
Jesus Christ our Lord.

Bill Lynn

266. **For prisoners**
Lord, who offers freedom to all people,
we pray for all who are in prison
and for those who are affected by,
or involved in their imprisonment.
Break the bonds of fear and isolation
and support with your love:
prisoners and their families and friends,
prison chaplains, prison staff and all who care.
Heal those who have been wounded
by the acts of others, especially victims of crime.
Help us to forgive one another, to act justly,
love mercy and walk humbly together with Christ.

William Davies

267. **Depressive illness**
We pray for the mentally ill,
for those whose spirits are tormented,
for those lost in the inner labyrinth of the mind.
May your spiritual light illuminate the valley of
shadows,
May your love lure them back from the far country,
May your angels bring them safely home
to a place of sunshine, peace and wholeness. Amen

Tom Stuckey

268. **Oil-rig workers**
Lord, who stilled the storm on Galilee,
we pray for those who, around the shores of many
countries
and in different climates, often endure danger on oil-rigs.
We pray for their wives and families
when they are separated for long periods of time;
and, when their future is uncertain,
may their faith be strengthened.
Grant them your guidance and peace
through the One whose peace no one can take away.

Lucy and Fred Valender

269. **Refugees**
God of all humanity
God of the wandering refugee
God who has nowhere to lay your head –
you hear the cries of cast-out people,
threatened, persecuted,
driven out by terror and cruel treatment,
out of their homes, their countries, their cultures . . .
you knock on the doors of the world
waiting to be welcomed, waiting to enter
a place you can call your home –
give us eyes to see you in strangers
tongues to speak welcome in other languages
ears to hear the refugees' story
minds to honour them for who they are
hearts to embrace them in one family.
God who has nowhere to lay your head
God of the wandering refugee
God of all humanity. Amen

John Murray, Aotearoa New Zealand

270. God, Creator of one human family,
Jesus, Refugee from Herod's persecution,
Spirit of God, Comforter of all in need –
grant hope to all who, in fear and perplexity,
seek asylum. May those who are alone,
bereaved, or separated by distance from loved ones,
know your unfailing, compassionate care.
Give understanding to those from whom they seek
refuge,
that they may not suffer rejection,
indignity and disillusionment.
Forgive all that we ourselves have contributed,
through ignorance, apathy and lack of support,
to the world's pain; and inspire all who govern
with an awareness of the dignity of each human being.
Strengthen our vision of a new heaven and a new earth,
where the gifts of each are seen as the riches of all,
and the needs of each as the poverty of all.

Nigel Gilson

271. **The gift of touch**
Creator God,
You made us in your image,
To love and be loved.
You gave us *eyes* to see
Those who need love and to be loved.
You gave us *ears* to hear
Those who cry for lack of love.
You gave us *voice* and *speech*
    to console those broken by rejection.
You gave us *touch* to bring without word
The warmth of recognition and understanding
to those who dwell alone in fear and sorrow.
Creator God,
Teach us the skills
of *seeing and listening,*
of *speaking and touching,*
for with these tools you gave us the power
to mirror your Love. Amen

Peter Fox

272. Lord, our light in darkness, our hope in despair,
our peace in struggle, our joy in sorrow,
our way when we are lost,
May your light shine in the very darkest places
    of our hearts and of the world,
May your hope touch the hearts of those in despair,
May your peace reach individuals
    and countries torn by war,
May your joy be known to those who mourn,
May those who are lost know you the Way,
and may we be channels of your light,
    your hope, your peace, your joy,
And lead others in the Way of your love. Amen

Margaret James

3. Working for justice and peace

273. Deliver us, O God, from politics without principles, from wealth without work, from pleasure without conscience, from knowledge without character, from commerce without morality, from worship without sacrifice and from science without humanity. Amen

Mahatma Gandhi, India (1869-1948)

274. We long for a world
that is both just
and compassionate . . .
where authority and love
are inextricably joined.

Kenneth Todd, Ireland

275. God our Father, graciously bless our countries and send your light and your truth to lead our peoples in the paths of justice and peace. Give wisdom to those who exercise authority in government. Remove all causes of contention and strife, heal the wounds caused by political unrest, and make us a God-fearing people, living together in love and concord, through Jesus Christ our Lord. Amen

Michael K Stephen, Nigeria

276. King of kings and Lord of lords, we thank you for all
who so generously give of themselves in public life.
We pray for those who govern us:
the Queen and the Royal Family,
the Prime Minister and his government,
and all who sit in Parliament.
Grant them patience in their deliberations,
intelligence in their framing of our laws,
compassion in the tactics they use,
and wisdom in the decisions they reach.
Heavenly Father, help all who exercise power
in the realm of politics
to walk humbly,
to temper justice with mercy,
and to seek the common good.
Cleanse our political life from all that tends to mere
sectional interest, character assassination or slander.
May all politicians be inspired by the noble ideal of
serving others.
In the name of him whose own supreme authority on
earth and in heaven flows from his readiness to serve,
even Jesus Christ our Lord. Amen

Leslie Griffiths

277. Heavenly Father, we praise you for your merciful
protection of all your people; you know our situation.
May your Holy Spirit enlighten those who govern us;
may human rights be respected; may your name be
honoured; may your will be done. In Jesus' name we
pray. Amen

Valentin Dedji, Benin

278. Compassionate God,
console us as we mourn loss
in our attempts to establish your common wealth.
Encourage us to continue the struggle
and accept us again as we fall at your feet.
In our success and failure,
strength and weakness,
life and death,
let us always seek your glory.

Israel Selvanayagam, Church of South India

279. Lord, all through the Bible – all through Church
history –
we hear about working for justice,
and helping the oppressed, and Jesus said,
'I come to bring good news to the poor.'
We struggle to follow Jesus in loving our neighbour.
Yet we know that in so many countries
thousands, even millions of children, are dying
because of the breakdown of health services;
and children are taught, 120 to a class,
if they can get to school at all.
Help us to get to the root of poverty:
to challenge structures and systems
that keep people poor, in bondage to debt,
while the rich world profits.
Lord, we thank you that throughout history
people have striven for justice,
getting rid of slavery and apartheid.
Show me now what you want me to do,
and give me the commitment to carry it through.

Gillian Weeks

280. O God, to those who are hungry give bread,
and to us, who have bread,
give hunger for justice.

Latin America

109

281. Gracious God, help us to live on a large map
      and fight poverty and injustice;
      challenge and inspire us
      to be the faith community you wish us to be
      and enfold us in your searching love.

Stuart Burgess

282. God of love, we pray for peace that brings true freedom
      because weapons have been transformed into tools for
          agriculture;
      for peace where people build houses and plant gardens
      and live to enjoy their fruits;
      where food grows and people celebrate the harvest;
      where children play and laugh;
      where all live without fear and, in thanksgiving,
      want to share the food and good things they produce.
      In the name of Christ, in whom is power to heal and
          save.

Maureen Edwards

283. God of mercy and hope,
          in the struggle for freedom grant us strength;
          in decisions about freedom grant us wisdom;
          in the practice of freedom grant us guidance;
          in the dangers of freedom grant us protection;
          in the life of freedom grant us joy
          and in the use of freedom grant us vision;
          for your name's sake. Amen

Latin American Council of Churches

284. Lord, we pray for all nations,
          that peace and justice may be known by every person.
          Let us not be bystanders only,
          but active ambassadors of the gospel
          which can renew our hearts, our lives
          and which makes us capable of love and pardon.

Valdo Benecchi, Italy

285. **Praying with women**
God our Creator, you make all people in your image.
We give thanks for the growing contribution of women
in church and society;
for the insights and changes they bring;
for their love and creativity, courage and strength:
(in silence name individuals or groups . . .).
Use them to transform your world.

Christ our Companion, you walk with us
wherever the road leads.
Hear our prayers for women who are ignored,
ridiculed, silenced, mutilated and killed:
(in silence name individuals or groups . . .).
Give them the knowledge of your unfailing love.

Spirit of truth, inflame us with your passion for justice
to challenge and confront sexism,
that we may support our sisters wherever they struggle;
and that we might dare to be ourselves,
reflecting your glory, now and for ever.

Carole Burgess

286. A candle light is a protest at midnight.
It is non-conformist.
It says to the darkness,
'I beg to differ.'

Samuel Rayan, India

287. God, Lord of history, many barriers still remain before
us.
Casting aside our arrogance, let us resolve all things
by wisdom and courage, prayer and faith.
So that our people may be tested no longer;
so that we may no longer be divided . . .
until at last God's Kingdom comes . . .
In the name of Jesus Christ we pray. Amen

National Council of Churches in Korea

288. Loving God, we rejoice with you
in the achievements of our towns and cities,
their architecture, industries and culture –
signs of vitality and opportunity.
We also weep with you at the widening gap
between rich and poor:
busy people overwhelmed by stress,
traffic congestion and pollution,
unemployed, homeless young people in Britain,
street children in Brazil,
women and men, isolated and forgotten,
crucified peoples . . .

Yet there you are; you share the pain,
and pierce the darkness with light and hope,
calling us to stand up for what is good,
and to wait upon and serve one another,
so that our polluted urban life may be transformed
into cities whose builder and maker is God.

Maureen Edwards

289. Gracious God,
let your presence be felt deep within our soul,
disturbing our tranquillity amid violence and injustice.
Remind us that words without actions
and Churches without a mission
are empty entities.
Open our hearts that we might respond to Jesus' call
to love and care for our neighbour.
Convince us that every person is made in your image.
Etch upon our minds
that when any one of your children is denied dignity,
all of us are denied life.
Send your Spirit, O God,
to teach us to love as Jesus loved.

Cathy Wimsatt, Argentina

290. When hope is weakened
      He comes to us and says
      Look at your sister who
      struggles for a better world
      Look at your brother
      committed to transforming life
      with blood and sweat.

      **Let us sing to our God,
      He is the Lord, God of life
      He gives us hope and came to
      this world to struggle with us.**

      When hope is weakened
      He comes to us and says
      Go find your sister to help her
      work for peace
      and unite in the struggle with
      your brother, for the life that
      remakes the world.

      When hope is weakened,
      He comes to us and says
      Stay close to me, keep firm
      and I will be firm too;
      Stay with me in the struggle,
      and I will give you strength
      and victory.

                                          Brazil

291. Dear Lord, forgive our timidity,
      and grant us by your Holy Spirit
      the power to accept one another as we are,
      and to love those who, but for you,
      we would see only as enemies.

                              Peter Good, Ireland

292. God, good beyond all that is good, fair beyond all that is fair, in you is calmness, peace and concord. Heal our divisions, draw us into your divine nature, and through the embrace of your love make us one in the Spirit. Amen

St Dionysius of Alexandria (3rd century)

293. Bless your people, Lord,
who have walked too long in this night of pain.
The cry from the cross is heard throughout the land.
The pain of your nailed hands is carried by the worker.
With your Spirit, Lord, we cry for peace.
With your Spirit, Lord, we struggle to be free.

National Council of Churches in the Philippines

294. O Saviour Christ,
Light of the world
and Prince of Peace:
give to those who pray
a longing for your Kingdom
of justice and love.
Grant to those who lead the nations
the true welfare of their people,
and to those at war
the wisdom of settlement and peace.
Take from our hearts
all greed, envy and pride
and equip your Church throughout the world
with the gift of prophetic speech
and the ministry of true reconciliation;
and this we ask
for your own name's sake. Amen

Norman Wallwork

295. O loving Lord,
      Our country needs justice for our security
          and mercy for our nurture.
      Thank you that in yourself you link justice with mercy
          and combine power with love.
      We long for a world that is both just and compassionate.
      We look for a world where authority and love
          are inextricably joined.
      Challenge your Church to reach beyond the barriers
          that we have created.
      Change your Church so that we look to the interests
          of others rather than our own.
      Cleanse your Church with the Spirit of holiness
          and renew us with Calvary love.
      Focus us on Kingdom values of righteousness,
          peace and joy.
      And by the grace of Christ, in the power of the Holy
          Spirit,
      We will ever live for your glory. Amen

                                    Kenneth Todd, Ireland

296. God of peace and serenity,
      bid the raging seas of the world's conflicts to be still.
      Transform all institutions of pride and domination
      into instruments of service for the poor and oppressed.
      Empower your Church to make sense of your presence
      as salt and light for the world,
      for, in the end, you are God,
      and in Christ you are our peace.

                                    Akuila Yabaki, Fiji

297. Lord God! We give you thanks
for sending your only Son to give us life . . .
Yet, in the midst of wealth, we are crushed by poverty,
and while we are offered Christ-life in all its fullness,
we are ever surrounded by disease, death and destruction.
We are tempted to despair, and yet keep hoping,
knowing that you care.
At times, when we are burdened by debt
and when our young people are confronted
    by many dangers,
we weep silent tears, and cry out with deep emotion.
We come to you, our only hope and refuge.
Help us, O God, to refuse to be embittered
Thank you for the gift of laughter,
even when the going is tough.
With you, O Lord, we may be troubled but not destroyed.

Farai Chirisa, Zimbabwe

298. Loving God, we thank you that you touch the lives
of countless people in the complex situations
and painful circumstances they face daily:
the ravages of nature,
the evil hand of wars,
the corruption of those in high places,
the resistance of the military to be held accountable
    for past crimes,
the deterioration of life caused by the present market
    system and external debt;
and yet you have made them resilient, hopeful
and determined to fight for life in all its fullness.
We pray for them in their struggle and ask
that we may join with them in a spirit of solidarity
so that, with them, we may glimpse your Kingdom
where love and peace and justice reign. Amen

Luis Veagra, Panama

299. Lord, we had hoped that we had found a way
    to resolve conflict without war;
we hoped that days such as these would never come
    again;
we hoped that the weapons that we manufacture
    would never be used.
We offer our shame for history we know little of,
for confusion of interests.
We offer our revulsion within the continuing tragedy of
    war;
we offer our grief for creation poisoned,
    for soldiers and civilians killed,
    for cities, towns, and villages destroyed,
    for families bereaved.
We offer the hurt and resentment
    that distorts our images of each other;
we offer our powerlessness in watching and waiting.
We offer our tension, longing and our hopes,
    not in gloom and despair but in confidence
    of God's forgiveness, mercy and healing.

Source unknown

300. Eternal God, as the rainbow spans the heavens when the
    clouds are dark, so our strifes and enmities stand under
    the judgement of your over-arching love and
    righteousness. We thank you for those who in former
    times were our enemies and are now our friends, and for
    the concern for peace which grows in the hearts and
    minds of ordinary people the world over. Use that
    concern to create the structures of peace and a new
    atmosphere of co-operation. Help us to identify the
    common enemies of all the nations and to work together
    for the eradication of poverty, hunger and disease. Give
    us the will to build defences against these instead of
    against each other, for the sake of Jesus Christ our
    Saviour.

Kenneth G Greet

301. We commit ourselves to deepen our inner lives
so that we will not fear the future.
We commit ourselves to renounce private forms of faith,
to live in communities of support and affirmation.
We commit ourselves to the way of non-violence,
cherishing forgiveness and reconciliation,
being prepared to suffer for the Kingdom.
We commit ourselves to develop solidarity
with our sisters and brothers in every land
who share with us the dream of shalom.
We commit ourselves to light candles in the dark,
to speak when all around are silent,
and to live the gospel in simplicity.
We commit ourselves to celebrate the promise of peace,
to nurture the spirit of festivity
and to grow in joy and expectation. Alleluia!

Christian Conference of Asia

302. From the land of Resurrection and the cradle of the
promise of salvation to all humankind through Jesus
Christ our Lord, and with a candle of hope, we pray to
you, God our Father, that the action of peace-seekers and
peace-makers may bear fruit so that
Hope will take the place of despair,
Justice will prevail over oppression,
Peace will turn strife into love.

Women's World Day of Prayer Committee, Jerusalem

303. God of love,
enfold the hurt and bereaved in your embrace.
God of joy,
with all creation we sing your praise.

God of peace,
heal the blindness of those who plan acts of terror.
God of hope,
your universal reign is coming!

Peter Good, Ireland

304. Almighty God, who brings good out of evil
and who transforms even the wrath of people into your
    praise,
we beseech you to bring lasting peace out of the present
    strife;
that we may be united in a new fellowship
telling of your glory and goodness,
so that all may experience the Kingdom of God on earth
through the power of the Holy Spirit.

Peter Kugba-Nyande, Sierra Leone

305. O God, Creator of all humankind, look with mercy upon
    us
and, in your great goodness, give us the peace, justice
and the unity for which we long.
Restrain those who plan evil
and encourage those who work for the common good.
Protect those who live in danger,
and those whose duty exposes them to harm.
Uphold those who suffer
and strengthen those who are afraid.
Temper, O Lord, our lifestyles with simplicity,
courage, humility and the love of the truth.

Lord Jesus Christ, our Brother on our way,
give peace to all those who disagree with us.
Take from us our fear of death,
and make us ready to walk beside you
and to love all people. We hope for your Kingdom
as we hope for peace.

Geetha de Chikera, Sri Lanka

306. **Bridge – a reflection**
When the word BRIDGE is heard, we immediately picture two sides that are joined together. It takes a lot of time and strength to build a bridge, because we need to get from one side to another; and yet, it takes only a few seconds to destroy it, because the joint is fragile. Years and years had passed before the bridge across the Danube connecting Petrovaradin and Novi Sad was built; only one well-targeted bomb was enough to destroy it for ever. A lot of energy was needed to unite two worlds by this bridge: the Orthodox world living on one side and the Catholic world living on the other – a single bomb managed to divide them.

Bridges are constructions that we are proud of, but at the same time, they are constructions of the spirit, which join people and objects. This is why the bridge in Novi Sad was not just a construction: it was a construction of emotions, since every citizen had somebody or something in the other part of the town. The pupils of the High School in Sremski Karlovci used to cross this bridge every day on their way to school. They were going to the other side to gain knowledge, find their first love and spend hours and days that were to remain a part of their youth memories. One bridge had disappeared – the bridge that connected the citizens of Petrovaradin and the three beautiful Catholic churches that their fellow citizens from Novi Sad used to visit once a day or week. Those who had their peaceful oases in the Fruska Gora Mountain cannot find their rest there any more. We, from here, cannot go to them who are over there – it hurts! This is why we protest!

The bombardment of the bridge in Novi Sad symbolises division between nations, parts of the world, the division within ourselves . . . Bridges are disappearing, the bridges that join us and remind us of the fact that it is possible to live together . . .

Svenka Savic, Novi Sad 2.4.1999

307. There's a time for healing, and a time for forgiving.
There's a time for building bridges, and that time is now.
O take our hearts, Lord, take our minds.
Take our hands, Lord, and make them one.

St George's Cathedral, Jerusalem

4. Caring for the earth

308. Dear God, our Creator,
You have made us in your image
to be like you in caring for one another,
for the land
and for the sea we share.

Today you call us:
'Where are you? What have you done?'
Silence

Forgive us for the sin of complicity
in over-valuing the power which corrupts
and destroys
and which, in our hypocrisy,
we often openly condemn.
Give us courage
to stand for the truth which sets people free;
to resist plans that could be harmful to your creation.

Call us yet again
to use the power you have given
to safeguard the gift of Life
and to be responsible stewards of it.

Restore to us
the joy of living in simplicity
and contentment with our environment.

Akuila Yabaki, Fiji

309. These words are written at a window
      overlooking a backyard
      on the industrial edge of a great city.
      The sounds of heavy traffic, by road and rail,
      planes overhead,
      power drills, TV laughter and electronic music
      almost drown the song of a blackbird on the chimney
            pot.

      There is a layer of grime on the sill,
      the air is heavy with fumes,
      yet in the yard grow roses and marigolds,
      geraniums and herbs.
      Blades of grass burst through the cracks of the paving,
      green leaves breathe a fresher air.

      People are at work, at odds with each other,
      anxious about their jobs, health, housing,
      they are angry and afraid –
      they do not have time to stand and see
      a sparrow ruffle its feathers in the sunlight on the wall.
      But God sees the sparrow fall – and fly –
      and on the wasteland thistles,
      a charm of goldfinches.

      God, our Creator,
      you daily rise in hope upon this imperfect world.
      May we see your creation with new eyes,
      and live that hope:

      'Daystar in our hearts appear!'

                                        Jan Sutch Pickard

310. Lord, what a wonderful world! Forgive us that we
            spoil it.
      Life is a precious possession: forgive us that we waste it.
      Love is the greatest gift: forgive us that we devalue it.
      Lord God, Creator, recall us to your purpose;
      Lord Jesus, Redeemer, renew in us your life;
      Spirit of the Living God, renew us with your gifts. Amen

                                        Michael Wearing

311. Come, Spirit of Wisdom,
     be that inner sense to be present in us
     for decisions hence.
     Come, Spirit of Vision,
     and give us sight to perceive your future
     and do what you might.
     Come, Spirit of Justice,
     set us on fire to stand up
     in all lands for what you desire.

Uniting Church of Australia

312. Spirit of creation, spilling into rivers and oceans,
     cleanse the life-giving waters.
     Spirit of creation, rushing through mighty forests,
     spread the seeds of new life.
     Spirit of creation, burning in the hearts of your people,
     give life, reborn and renewed.
     Spirit of God, water, wind and fire,
     fill us with your love. Amen

Diane Clutterbuck

313. Teach me to walk the soft earth as a relative to all that
     live.
     Sweeten my heart and fill me with light.
     Give me strength to understand and the eyes to see.

Black Elk, Ogala Sioux

314. Good and gracious God,
     we thank you for the rich diversity of life:
     may we respond with respect for the earth
     and for all your creatures,
     and with loving attention to human need,
     through Jesus Christ our Lord.

Peter Sulston

315. O God of earth and sky,
      of crashing waves and rolling plains,
      grant us eyes to behold you in the wonders of creation
      and give us the will to protect this fragile planet
      which is our home.
      O Christ, redeemer and hope-bringer,
      who came to us from the dirt, chaos and mess of
            creation,
      you give shelter to the lost,
      release to those shackled by pain,
      and you bring light to dwellers in darkness;
      may your Kingdom come.
      O Spirit of God, giver of life and mother of birth,
      restore our connectedness with each other,
      blow through our churches
      with your renewing wind of change,
      and enable the barren wilderness places of our hearts
      to blossom as a rose.

Tom Stuckey

316. We pray:
      for those who make decisions about the earth's
            resources,
      that we may use your gifts responsibly;
      for those who work on the land and sea, in city and in
            industry,
      **that all may enjoy the fruits of their labours and
      marvel at your creation;**
      for artists, scientists and visionaries,
      that through their work we may see creation afresh.
      We thank you that you have called us to celebrate your
            creation.
      Give us reverence for life in your world.

Aotearoa New Zealand

317. The tree, dependent on the soil in which it grows,
a home for animals, birds and insects,
fungi and other parasites, the beautiful orchid . . .
Absorbing the impurities of the air we breathe
and giving out oxygen,
it heals and gives life to the world.
Fragile, it can be broken and smashed by wind and
hurricane,
but in the process of falling to the ground and dying,
it gives life again to the soil that nourished it.
Trees hold the land together and save it from becoming a
desert,
shedding leaves to be broken down by the forces of
nature
to renew the earth.

Creating God, trees speak to us of the mystery
of your presence, and your words to us:
'I created you. I love you and care for you.
You belong to me like branches of the tree.
My name is Emmanuel.
I will be with you until the end of time and beyond
with all the energy and love that are needed to heal
and nourish the nations and their peoples;
and to bring all things into a unity in Christ.'

Creator God, help us to care for the trees
which you planted that we may have abundant life.

Maureen Edwards

318. Creator God,
you made the wells of this earth and continue
to replenish them.
You send rain on the righteous and on the unrighteous
and invite us to drink the water of life.
We pray for all lands which cry out for rain,
that they may be blessed.
We pray also for those places where floods destroy.
May we thirst until we find a vital harmony with the
earth,
replenished and whole.
To you we turn.

World Council of Churches

319. Every part of this earth is sacred,
     every shining pine needle, every sandy shore,
     every mist in the dark woods,
     the beasts and all the people.
     All belong to the same family.
     The earth is our mother. Whatever befalls the earth
     befalls the children of the earth.
     We are part of the earth and the earth is part of us.
     The rivers are our brothers; they quench our thirst.
     The perfumed flowers are our sisters.
     The air is precious, for all of us share the same breath.
     This we know, the earth does not belong to us:
     we belong to the earth.
     This we know, all things are connected.
     **Our God is the same God, whose compassion is for
     all.**
     We did not weave the web of life:
     We are merely a strand in it.
     Whatever we do to the web
     we do to ourselves.
     Let us give thanks for the web
     and the circle that connects us.
     Thanks be to God, the God of all.

     Adapted litany drawn from the writings of Chief Seattle (1854)

320. Source of all being, whom Christ called 'Father',
     supreme among your many gifts to us
     is the capacity to love.
     Increase in us, we pray, the quality of our loving
     so that we may care for and comfort one another.
     Extend our loving to all creation so that we may be
     caring stewards of our beautiful earth.
     This we ask in the name of Jesus Christ
     who taught and showed us the way to love.

     Dorothy Bimrose

321. God, the promise of life in unfurling poppy petals,
       spreading butterfly wings,
       bursting buds,
       and tiny, trusting hands,
 give us sensibility
  that we may learn to think fragility;
  understanding
  that we may know our part
  in the intricate pattern of being;
  companionship
  that we may live gently and simply
 alongside all living things.

 Give us eyes big with wonder
  that we may truly see
  the small things of our earth;
  ears sharp to hear
  what lies on the other side of silence;
  hearts of flesh that we may feel beauty.
 For what we truly see, hear and feel,
 we will not pollute, exploit or destroy,
 but will care for tenderly.
 We will cherish this fragile and finite planet
 which is our only home,
 and know the holiness of becoming
 fully and integrally human.

Joy Mead

322. Gracious God . . .
 Let all be partners in shaping the future
 with a faith that quarrels with the present
 for the sake of what yet might be.

Taiwan

IV

Our Calling – Making Followers

1. We have a gospel to proclaim

323. Creator, Redeemer and Saviour God, in you is the fullness of goodness, mercy and gentleness. You alone are just and holy, innocent and pure. Only in you is all pardon, all grace and all glory, without beginning and without end. Amen

St Francis of Assisi (1181-1226)

324. Draw us, O Christ, by grace irresistible, to the centre of all faith and to the heart of all sacrifice; to the deepest of all wells and to a work that is not our own; even your Holy Cross, to which we cling and by which we are held; for your own name's sake. Amen

Dora Greenwell (1821-1882)

325. Gracious God, we thank you for your Son Jesus Christ
who became a human being so that we may have life.
Help your Church to continue to seek that fullness of life
which is found in Jesus and is for all people.
At the beginning of the third millennium,
open our eyes to see you making 'all things new'
for us as individuals, communities and the world.

Stephen and Mercy Abakah, Ghana

326. O God,
     what abundant reason I have to adore,
     to praise,
     and to magnify your goodness
     and love for sending your Son
     into the world to die for sinners.
     What reason have I to praise,
     adore and love that Saviour who
     suffered so much to redeem me . . .

     How gladly and cheerfully
     should I take up my cross
     for you who suffered death
     upon the Cross for me.
     Help me to praise and adore the blessed Spirit
     Who sanctifies and illumines my mind;
     Who co-operates with the means of grace;
     and who condescends
     to visit, assist and refresh my weary soul
     by his powerful influences.
     Glory be to the Father, Son and Holy Spirit!
     Joint authors of my salvation! Amen

Susanna Wesley (1669-1742)

327. O Good Shepherd, seek me and search for me, and bring
     me home again to your fold. Deal tenderly with me and
     anoint me with your grace that I may dwell in your house
     all the days of my life and praise you with your saints for
     ever and ever. Amen

St Jerome (c.342-420)

328. Lord, you give us a task to fulfil,
     a message to proclaim,
     a love to share.
     Surprise us by answering our prayers! Amen

John G Mitchell

131

329. Lord Jesus, you have called your Church to announce
      good news in your name, forgiveness, hope, a new
      heaven and a new earth; to denounce powers and
      principalities, sin and injustice; to console widows and
      orphans, restore the broken-hearted, comfort the
      sorrowful; and to celebrate life in the midst of death.

      In faithfulness we follow you, bringing our hearts, minds
      and wills to your altar, knowing that from worship comes
      wisdom, from prayer comes strength and from fellowship
      comes endurance for the task. Amen

                                        Lesley G Anderson, Panama

330. O God of light and life and love,
      by your Spirit help us to live the truth:
      Your light is stronger than darkness.
      Your life means more than death,
      Your love can overcome all things.
      May the light of Christ shine in us and through us,
      May the life of Christ free us for proper living,
      May the love of Christ control us;
      We ask this for your glory,
      O God of life and light and love. Amen

                                        Kenneth Hext

331. Jesus, our Saviour,
      we thank you for love shown in action:
      for your coming to be one with us,
      for the way you taught and healed,
      let yourself be accused and hurt,
      suffered for us on the cross,
      and showed us, on Easter Sunday,
      that love is stronger than death.

                                        Jan Sutch Pickard

332. Dear God, your amazing love embraces all humanity
and the world you have created.
We thank you for your presence,
encouragement, hope and sustaining grace
in the midst of human suffering.
Give us renewed courage and faith
to participate with you in your liberating mission.
Teach us to love as Jesus did;
to be in solidarity
with those who are not able to develop their potential
because of abuse, discrimination, injustice, or
deprivation.
Empower your Church
to proclaim the good news of abundant life
with boldness, faith and conviction;
to fulfil its prophetic role in our own time and context;
in Jesus' name. Amen

Saray Veagra, Panama

333. Great God of love, we rejoice
to see your love revealed in the life, death and
resurrection
of Jesus Christ your Son,
and to know that love is for everyone.
May our discovery of your treasure become a gift we
share
to the honour of your name.
(Based on Hymns & Psalms 45)

David Reddish

334. Lord Jesus Christ, make me today a gossip of the gospel.
Help me to share good news with those who are
low-spirited,
to speak words of comfort to those who are broken-
hearted,
to give hope of freedom to those who are oppressed,
and to remind those who despair of our world
that you have come into it,
so that through your love the world might be saved.
May all my words and actions help to convince others
that they are loved by you, for your sake. Amen

Pauline Webb

335. Grant us, God our Father, the knowledge of your forgiveness, your gift of new life, the vision of your Kingdom and the stirring of your Spirit, that we may proclaim your love, share your gifts and change this world, in the name of Christ our Lord. Amen

Martin Evans Jones

336. Lord Jesus, we thank you that you provide for us not only physical bread to eat, but also spiritual food for us to be strengthened to stand up and witness for you.
Lord, provide for your people wherever they are. Amen

Gershon Anderson, Sierra Leone

337. Creator God,
as new buildings and witness arise from dust and decay,
help us to focus on you
and your mission – not our own –
for this ever-changing world.
As stones and bricks are laid down,
let the first one in all we do be yours,
for you are the Cornerstone
and the Rock
upon which we must stand. Amen

Diane Allen, USA

338. Deliver us, O Lord,
from the preaching that does not challenge our pleasures;
from the praying that does not challenge our priorities;
and from the praising that does not challenge our
politics;
for Jesus' sake. Amen

Norman Wallwork

339. God, our Father, we praise you for the vision of your
          love
    in the life and death of Jesus Christ –
    a love for all, even though we do not deserve it
      and have often rejected it;
    a love that forgives our past failures
      and offers a new beginning;
    a love that goes on loving, giving itself to us
      without reserve and without condition.
    May the vision of your love capture anew our lives
    and the lives of all for whom we pray.

    As we remember the love of Jesus
        for his family and friends –
        thinking of Mary and John, not himself,
        when he was dying -
    we pray for our families and friends,
    especially those who have lost the capacity to give
        and forgive.
    Renew their sense of the self-giving love of Jesus,
    and help them to receive and share it.
    May the vision of your love capture anew our lives
    and the lives of all for whom we pray.

    As we remember the love of Jesus for his apostles,
    even when they denied and deserted him –
    we pray for his ministers today,
    especially those in unresponsive and unsupportive
        congregations.
    Renew, sustain and deepen their service
        among your people.
    May the vision of your love capture anew our lives
    and the lives of all for whom we pray.

    May the Spirit of Jesus draw us anew
        to trust and love you,
    liberating us from self-concern to love and serve others.

    Peter Stephens

340. Extravagant God, who welcomes us home
when we have drifted away from the path of goodness
to explore obscure areas of life,
we thank you that you search the horizon,
hoping for our return
and, when we do come back,
you run to meet us with open arms.
Before we can even ask you for pardon,
you embrace us and dance with those in heaven
and on earth
in celebrating our homecoming.

Luis Veagra, Panama

341. Lord our God, help us to love the unlovely, to tolerate the intolerant, to listen with patience, and to tell with confidence the story of Jesus; for his sake. Amen

Laurie Campbell

342. Lord God Almighty, save us from living as if Jesus had never been; as if there is no truth for us to share with others, no hope to lead us into the future, no inner power to bring strength in our weakness. Transform us day by day through the grace of the One who is the Way, the Truth, the Life, even Jesus Christ our Lord. Amen

Richard G Jones

343. Glory to God our creator, the Lord of heaven and earth, the preserver of all things. Glory to the Father of all mercies who, for our redemption, sent into the world his only-begotten Son, our Saviour Jesus Christ. Glory to God, the fire of holy love, pouring forth the life-giving glory of the Holy Spirit. Blessing and praise to God, Father, Son and Holy Spirit, now and for ever. Amen

John Hamilton (1512-71)

2. Sharing Faith

344.   Dear God, we thank you that all over the world
       people come to worship you with songs of praise.
       We thank you for sending your Son;
       for your love displayed by him
       through whom people of every nation come to you
       and enjoy fellowship together.
       In Jesus you called your Church into being,
       to proclaim your name everywhere and always.
       Move your people to respond, that through your Church,
       people near and far may hear your good news
       and delight in the citizenship of your Kingdom.

Roberta Mettle-Nunoo, Ghana/United Kingdom

345.   May the risen Lord grant us the power of his
            resurrection,
       transform us to be his messengers,
       instil in us a new spirit to go out into the world
       and boldly proclaim the good news
       that the Lord has risen indeed. Amen

Vasant P Dandin, Church of South India

346. Thanks be to you, O God, for all your gifts . . .
      Thank you for placing us here, at this time,
      to be bearers of the good news of your Son, Jesus Christ.
      Holy Spirit, breath of life, energise your body the
          Church,
      that we may be faithful witnesses
      in our land and in the world.

Farai Chirisa, Zimbabwe

347. We give thanks for those who are challenging
      congregations to put Jesus at the centre; for those who are
      teaching members to share their faith.
      We pray that all who are engaged in this mission will be
      encouraged and supported in their work. May the whole
      Church take seriously the need to pray for those without
      Christ, that many may come to know Jesus. Help us to
      grow in joy and expectancy as we hear the gospel
      proclaimed and see people respond.

Linda Ashford

348. Father, we pray that needs may be identified and met;
      that opportunities for evangelisation and ecumenical
      witness may be grasped; that relationships with those of
      other faiths and those of no faith may be deepened, and
      all for the sake of Jesus Christ our Lord.

Michael Wearing

349. Draw your Church, O Lord, into one great company of
      disciples, together following our Lord Jesus Christ into
      every walk of life, together serving him in his mission to
      the world, and together witnessing to his love on every
      continent and island. We ask this in his name and for his
      sake. Amen

Canada

350. Eternal God,
      whose love created us and constantly sustains us,
      we, your children, rejoice in this life-giving relationship,
      and in the invitation you offer us
      to join in your mission to rescue the world.
      Give us grace to recognise that we ourselves
      need first to be rescued,
      for we confess that too readily
      we discern the 'speck' of trivial mistakes in others
      and ignore the 'plank' of our own deep sinfulness.

      By your gentle correcting, make us worthy
      so that, being made better and fully loved,
      we may be more effective
      in playing our part in your on-going, life-saving
          purposes.
      For, in our better moments,
      we want to reflect more truly
      the love we have discovered to be the heartbeat
      of creation.

      As we see more of Jesus,
      may we discover our real selves.
      Challenged by his life and death,
      may we serve selflessly as he did.
      To God, whose love redeems us,
      to Christ, whose grace transforms us,
      and to the Holy Spirit, whose power enables us,
      be honour, praise and glory for ever. Amen

Brian Thornton

351. Lord, help us to become transparent,
      opening, for the world, windows to Jesus;
      and may friend and stranger be for us
      icons of your otherness and love. Amen

Jan Sutch Pickard

352. Father God,
      Show us the relationship between commission and grace.
      We are called to share our faith
      But we confess
      That when we hear your compelling call
      We are sometimes paralysed by guilt and lack of
          confidence.
      Help us, Lord,
      To be so overwhelmed by the gospel of your love
      In the cross of Jesus,
      And to be so full of the Spirit,
      That the call to evangelise becomes an 'idiocy' –
      Or like being urged to breathe.
      I can't stop telling what the Lord has done!
      It pours out through my whole life.
      Let it be like that, Lord.
      Show us Jesus' method of mission,
      As much about being as doing,
      Multi-faceted – meeting people on their turf,
      Alongside the rich and the poor,
      Touching the untouchable,
      Saying the unthinkable,
      Ripping through the paraphernalia of religion
      With the word of truth.
      Instigating a way of being Church that is alive –
      More a movement than an institution.
      Travelling hopefully,
      Living riskily 'on the edge'
      Offering grace not condemnation,
      Welcoming all to the Kingdom party.

      Take me out of my comfort zone, Lord.
      Show me the doors of opportunity
      And give me the wit and the grace to go through them.
      Grant me courage to tell my story,
      To tell the story,
      And to trust you for harvest.

                                              Phil Clarke

353. Lord God Almighty, we praise and thank you for the many countries where people are responding eagerly to your gospel; for people who, in need and despair, turn to Christ for salvation, strength and courage.

We pray that your Church may be so filled with your Spirit, that we may preach your Word fearlessly, care for the needy and seek your guidance in all that we try to do in your name.

We pray for a return to Christian values of honesty, compassion, sexual morality, and for integrity, justice and humility in the lives of all national and Church leaders.

Farai Chirisa, Zimbabwe

354. Lord Jesus Christ, help our churches
to grow from strength to strength;
knowing that the good work you started in the beginning
will surely grow.
Give us, we pray, your burning fire
in our lives, that we may seek you more. Amen

Joshua Sambou, The Gambia

355. **Mission partners**
Loving God,
we rejoice in your boundless creativity
evident in every aspect of this your world;
especially we thank you that, created in your image,
each of us is unique.
We pray for your Church throughout the world
in all its diversity,
and thank you for the men and women whom you call
to serve you across boundaries of nation and culture.
We pray for our mission partners working in
other countries.
Through the international channels that they open for us,
may your Spirit inspire us anew
to work for your Kingdom to come on earth.

Gabrielle Grace

356. Let us pray for all whom Christ sends as his apostles, that they may witness to the gospel of resurrection. Lord, let your ways be known on earth;
Your saving power among the nations.
Let us pray for all whom Christ calls to be his prophets, that they may open the eyes of the blind to the gospel of righteousness and peace. Lord, let your ways be known on earth;
Your saving power among the nations.
Let us pray for all whom Christ calls to be his teachers, that they may lead Christians to understand the gospel and its meaning for today. Lord, let your ways be known on earth;
Your saving power among the nations.
Let us pray for all whom Christ calls to be his evangelists, that they may lead those outside the Church to fullness of life through the gospel. Lord, let your ways be known on earth;
Your saving power among the nations.
Let us pray for all whom Christ calls to be pastors and shepherds, that they may live the gospel life of caring and self-giving love. Lord, let your ways be known on earth;
Your saving power among the nations.
Let us pray for all whom Christ calls to be his healers and helpers, that their gospel hands may be signs and agents of the Kingdom of heaven. Lord, let your ways be known on earth;
Your saving power among the nations.

Norman Wallwork

357. By the grace of God we are a pilgrim people, ever moving forward and never settling down with the status quo. We bring our commitment to unity and mission, sharing with all the fullness of the blessing of the good news of Jesus Christ.
Holy God, fill us with the power of your Spirit that we may be your witnesses to the ends of the earth. Amen

Church of South India

358. Creating Word,
     bringing the world into being,
     for the starred sky and the songbird that tell of your
         being,
     for peoples diverse in colour and culture,
     made in your image, speaking in many tongues –
     we praise you.
         Help us to see you at work in the world:
         May our lives tell the Good News.

     Living Word,
     seen and heard in Jesus, teacher and storyteller,
     speaking words of healing and forgiveness,
     standing silent in the face of hatred and lies,
     crying out on the cross –
     we believe in you.
         Help us to hear the cries of the world today:
         May our lives tell the Good News.

     Breath of the Spirit,
     rushing wind and still small voice,
     challenging, changing, making connections,
     creating community, encouraging hope,
     come among us, inspire us –
     we need you.
         Help us to communicate your love:
         May our lives tell the Good News.

     Jan Sutch Pickard

359. Lord, may your people in every country reach out
     to all who need the gospel of our Lord Jesus Christ,
     that all may hear and know Jesus as Lord and Saviour.
     May the wind of the Holy Spirit blow across
     the continents and oceans
     so that many may see the salvation of our Lord.

     Tomasi Kanailagi, Fiji

360. God of love,
increase in us an awareness of the Spirit
who leads us forward across new boundaries,
to discover Christ
in all whom we encounter.
Make us sensitive to the spirit of honest enquiry.

Maureen Edwards

361. Loving Lord Jesus,
grant us your vision,
make clear your will,
and enable us to obey
and serve you
in the power of the Holy Spirit. Amen

Thomas Kingston, Ireland

362. O God, who in Jesus Christ revealed your love for all
people, help us in everything we say and do to express
that divine love, sharing the good news with conviction,
openness and sensitivity; by the leading and enabling
power of your Holy Spirit. Amen

Roger Ducker

363. Surrendering ourselves to your love, O God,
May we be spent doing the work of Christ,
All sharing and caring, teaching and learning,
Witnessing and praying
In the power of the Holy Spirit,
So that those far and near may be loved
Into your family. Amen

Methodist Church, Zimbabwe

364. O Holy Spirit, our liberator and comforter,
we are thankful that you have renewed us,
and given us courage
and new confidence.
Help us recapture our sense of mission
and share in your ministry of reconciliation.
Help us rediscover how to enrich the world
with your justice, peace and love.
Strengthen us that we may stand firm
against all forms of domination,
exploitation,
discrimination.

Strengthen us that we may meet the challenges
and opportunities of the present age
to proclaim with urgency:
'Good News to the poor,
liberty to the captives,
recovery of sight to the blind,
freedom for the oppressed,
and to announce the year when the Lord
will save his people' *(Luke 4:18,19).*

Strengthen us that we may move ahead,
out of the paths of divisiveness,
hopelessness,
powerlessness.

Strengthen us that we may go into the world
with your power to fulfil our calling
as servants of our Lord and Saviour Jesus Christ. Amen

Lesley G Anderson, Panama

365. Lord Jesus, give us today:
love in our meetings with others,
boldness in our sharing of your good news,
power in our activity for your Kingdom,
joy in worship and peace in your presence. Amen

Ian White

366. Lord God,
    as those who are called to be your witnesses today,
    we pray that we may bear witness by what we are,
    by what we do and by what we say.
    Give us true holiness of character,
    a deeper understanding of people and their needs,
    a love that is humble, outgoing and open.
    So may our lives reflect something of your grace and
        truth
    made known to us in Jesus Christ our Lord. Amen

Aian Ferguson, Ireland

367. O God, Trinity of unity and love,
    we hear you calling us
    to leave behind the divisions of the past
    and find our true unity in you.
    Forgive our fears and faithlessness,
    open our eyes to your future for your Church,
    and give us the strength and courage
        to turn the vision into reality,
    that together we might reveal
    your redeeming love to our land. Amen

Scottish Church Initiative for Union

368. Lord, deepen our understanding of your nature;
    increase in us the awareness of your ways.
    Draw us into those paths that lead to the transforming
    both of nations and of people.
    Strengthen us in our weakness,
    hold us in our trembling,
    and form us into the stewards of your mysteries,
    through Christ our Lord. Amen

Donald Eadie

369. Make us communities of love,
    that are strong enough, and
    open enough, to include others. Amen

World Village

370. Lord, sometimes we are sad
 and get discouraged when our church buildings are
  empty
 apart from the devoted, faithful few.
 Cast away our fears and remove our doubts.
 Increase our faith and inspire us through your Holy Spirit
 to see the direction of your Church at this time.
 Lord, give us wisdom and shelter us with your peace,
 so that we may not turn away
 from your calling in Jesus Christ,
 and that you may complete through us
 that which you have called us to do.
 Through Jesus Christ our Lord.

Martin K Freeman, Liberia

371. **Bridges of love**
 God of love, who enfolds all the world in one embrace,
 help us, your people, to build bridges of love:
 Bridges between young and old,
 poor and rich,
 black and white;
 bridges between those who know you
 and those who do not yet know you,
 bridges between traditionalists and modernisers,
 between nations and within communities.
 As in your self-giving, life-giving love for us,
 you became, in Jesus Christ, the Bridge
 between heaven and earth,
 so may we become bridges of the gospel.
 When we are walked over, give us courage;
 when we are taken for granted, give us grace;
 when we are despised, give us strength –
 so that through our lives
 others may catch a glimpse of Jesus the Redeemer,
 and entrust themselves to your saving mercy.
 God of love, hear our prayer,
 through Jesus, our Lord and Saviour.

Margaret Parker

372. At the beginning of the new Millennium –
     in a troubled world, influenced by secularism
     and plagued by brokenness and pressing human need –
     we ask you, dear God, to instruct, guide and empower
     the Churches in Britain and Ireland with your Holy Spirit
     to encourage the reading and study of your Word;
     to proclaim the gospel with renewed faith,
     boldness and effectiveness.
     Enable ordinary Christians to lead people to Jesus Christ,
     so that, in him and through him, they may find
     new meaning and purpose for the present and future.

     Luis and Saray Veagra, Panama

373. Loving God, empower your Church in Britain and
     Ireland to tell 'your story' with new vigour and meaning,
     in a new distinct way that says, 'We belong together.'
     Give us a new love for you and one another. In a
     partnership of creativity and vision that can make a
     difference wherever we are, and in all we encounter, we
     entrust the future to your guidance.

     Tevita and Meleane Siuhengalu, Netane,
     Taulama and Louisa, Tonga

374. O God of love and mercy, your Son Jesus Christ has
     commanded us to preach and teach and baptise people in
     Jesus' name. Help us to carry out this great commission
     with humble hearts. Amen

     William To Kilala, Solomon Islands

375. Calling and sending God,
     create in each and all of us a clear sense of vocation,
     that we may be a truly missionary congregation,
     rejoicing together in the variety of gifts
     you have planted in us – that the world may believe.

     Peter Whittaker

376. Loving God,
    whose glory is shown in the beauty of Creation
    and in Christ,
    be glorified in your Church.
    Make us strong by your Holy Spirit that,
    inspired by the nail prints of sacrifice,
    we may follow in the footprints of Christ,
    that others may come to know and love you.

    Kenneth Todd, Ireland

377. Dear Lord,
    help us not to lose heart when we are small minorities,
    and to recognise that our greatest strength lies in our
        weakness.
    Save us from preoccupation with our own safety or
        survival.
    Free us, unimpeded by power struggles,
    simply to obey you by witnessing and serving.
    Teach us how to be lowly vines, slender, struggling, yet
        fruitful.
    Show us how to be lamps, small yet shining brightly
        on tall lamp-stands:
    Poor ourselves, may we bring wealth to many. Amen
    Based on Genesis 49:22, Matthew 5:14-16
    and 2 Corinthians 6:10

    Norman Taggart, Ireland

378. Jesus still says, 'Fear not!'
    Lord Jesus, may we know the comfort of these words
    when the 'big wide world' attracts and distracts
    and we feel inadequate to proclaim you as Saviour.
    Lord Jesus, may we know the challenge of these words
    when you call us in a fast-changing world
    to new ways of witness and service.
    'Fear not, I am with you always.'

    Peter Good, Ireland

379. God of all creation and Lord of all history, let us never believe that we hold you as a possession. Remind us that relationship with you comes as a gift and that we are part of a larger plan to redeem your whole world. Amen

Melvyn Tarbert, United Methodist Church, USA

380. We give thanks for those wrestling
       with new ways of being 'Church';
       with new ways of announcing the gospel.
   At the same time, we give thanks
   for ordinary, everyday, bread and butter ministries:
       for those who offer welcome,
       for those who offer care and encouragement,
       for those who make our buildings beautiful,
       for those who polish
           and those who arrange the flowers,
       for those who offer transport . . .
   We pray for churches left without ordained ministry,
   that their members may discover their own ministries
   and allow their gifts to flourish.

John Taylor

381. Great God, who has been revealed to us in Jesus Christ, we thank you for the variety all around us: scenes of natural beauty and the races of people out of whom this nation has been created. May the work of mission undertaken in your name serve to bring people everywhere to acknowledge you as Creator and, through entering into your mission, may we also be brought closer to you.

Philip Robinson, Jamaica

382. Lord, I do hear you calling me, but I am not sure when or how or where to answer. Convince me that now is the right time for me to respond, show me the work you have chosen for me, and send me to the place of your appointment. Then in obeying your will may I find peace of mind. Amen

Pauline Webb

383. Lord, in obedience to your command to launch out into the deep, we have dared to venture. We thank you that your unerring Spirit is always with us. Amen

Wycherley Gumbs, Caribbean

384. Calling God,
    we give thanks that your call
    to share your gift of Jesus Christ
    comes to the whole Church.

    Empowered by your Holy Spirit,
    may the lives of each member
    of every congregation
    speak of Jesus as good news.

    We pray that all who hear
    and receive this good news
    will be filled
    with your glorious new life.

William Prince

3. Commitment

385. Take possession of our hearts, O Lord, that being created by you, we may ever live for you; that being created for you, we may ever act for your glory; and being redeemed by you, we may ever render to you what is yours. Amen

John Wesley (1703-91)

386. Take possession of our hearts, O Lord, and subdue them wholly to yourself. Fill our minds with pictures of your love, that within us there may be no room for thoughts discordant with your holy will. May we not be slow to hear your call or to obey it; for the sake of your only Son, our Saviour Jesus Christ. Amen

William Temple (1881-1944)

387. Gracious Father,
your love knows no limits.
Fill our hearts with your compassion,
open our eyes to your presence in the world,
enlarge our minds to understand your will.
Take our hands and minister through them.
Speak through our words
and direct our feet in the paths of peace,
that Christ may be revealed in us
and the world may believe.

David Reddish

388.   Lord Jesus, I give you my hands to do your work. I give you my feet to walk in your way. I give you my eyes to see the world as you see it. I give you my tongue to speak your praise and I give you myself that you may live and pray in me.

Lancelot Andrewes (1555-1626)

389.   Gracious God,
give us courage and humility to face the future.
Lord, hear us:
Lord, graciously hear us.
May we proclaim the good news of the gospel of Jesus Christ to all.
Lord, hear us:
Lord, graciously hear us.
May we be committed to peace and justice and to help the poor in the world.
Lord, hear us:
Lord, graciously hear us.
May we engage with the challenges of society and listen especially to young people.
Lord, hear us:
Lord, graciously hear us.
May we be committed to a faith journey with other Christians and respond positively to ecumenical initiatives.
Lord, hear us:
Lord, graciously hear us.
May we embrace in your love those whose lives are broken and shattered.
Lord, hear us:
Lord, graciously hear us.
May we dream dreams, take risks for the gospel's sake, and be inspired by your love for us.
In Christ's name. Amen

Stuart Burgess

390. Loving God, we thank you
      for differences of culture.
      May the rich experience of the old,
      the vibrancy of the young
      and the rainbow talents of all
      be joyfully put at your disposal for the sake of love.

                                            Colin Wilson

391. Heavenly Father, your commitment to me in Christ is
          total.
      Thank you for the assurance
      that nothing in all creation or human experience
      will ever be able to separate me from your love in Jesus.
      I really want to have a deeper sense of your love,
      a greater awareness of your presence,
      and a growing assurance of your peace in my life;
      that I may serve you more effectively
      in my church and local community
      and among my family, friends and neighbours,
      for Christ's sake. Amen

                                Ian D Henderson, Ireland

392. Lord, keep us near your cross
      and fill your people with Calvary love.
      Give courageous leadership to your Church,
      to speak the truth in love and to outlove its enemies.
      Anoint your Church afresh
      with the spirit of joyous, faithful service
      and let us seek only your glory. Amen

                                Kenneth Todd, Ireland

393. **A vocation to martyrdom**
The church of the poor in Brazil has received the gift of martyrdom. As martyrs for the cause of justice, and enriched with joy and courage, they carry and offer their gift to the World Church.

Lord, as I live today, give me the courage
to face the dangers of suffering and death,
as if I was a fearless person, full of faith,
faith that will bring change and lasting love.

Lord, as I live today, give me wisdom
to live as calmly as if it was not my last day,
as if I was to be alive in every person, every day
as we offer ourselves to achieve similar goals.

Lord, as I live today, give me the strength
to fight for righteousness and real peace
as if I was going to see for myself
the outcome of justice flowing like a river.

Lord, as I live today, give me grace
to welcome and forgive the ones who persecute and kill
as if I was going to be given the opportunity
to see open arms and love prevail.

Lord, as I live today, I am ready to live joyfully
holding tightly to your promises of abundant life
here and beyond. Amen

Reynaldo Leao, Brazil

394. Loving Father, we are humbled when we hear of those
who, through trial and tribulation, stand firm on the truth
of the gospel and place their loyalty to you higher than
their material or physical gain. We pray that in the hour
of testing we, too, may draw on your limitless resources,
through Christ. Amen

United Church of Zambia

395. Lord, remind us of the truth
that if we would be as lights in the world
we must endure the burning.

The Philippines

396. Loving God, by your grace
may our weakness become your strength,
our problems become your opportunities
and our defeats your victories;
so that the life of Jesus may be seen in our lives
and your name be glorified in all our days;
through Jesus Christ our Lord.

Michael Townsend

397. Gracious Father,
grant us wisdom to discern your purpose for the Church,
courage and will to perform it
for the salvation of all people.

Gilbert Hall

398. **The liberating touch**
In my hurry, Lord, I brush by some
and our lives do not touch at all.
In my concern, Lord, I reach out to some
but because of where I stand
they receive no helping hand.
In my need, Lord, some reach out to me
but because I shrink away,
our hands never touch.

Lord, you always come to all and to me
with your healing, liberating touch.
So touch my life with your love,
that I may be, each day, your out-stretched hand
of welcome and of love.

Kenneth Hext

399. Lord, you have promised in your Word
that those who wait upon you will renew their strength.
As we pray for and await the renewing of your Church,
may the Holy Spirit touch my life
to challenge me to greater commitment –
to break down the barriers of suspicion and mistrust in
me,
to heal the hurts that affect my life,
to forgive my sins of neglect
and enable me to acknowledge my need of grace and
love.

Ian D Henderson, Ireland

400. Lord of the way, the truth and the life
quicken our steps to walk in your ways,
illuminate our minds and hearts to understand your truth
and empower our lives with your overflowing life.

Brian Fletcher, Ireland

401. Sovereign Lord, enable us to be
gracious towards people who are different from us,
compassionate to the needy,
and courageous in presenting Jesus Christ
as Lord and Saviour of all.

Gilbert Hall

402. Lord God, may your Church be as a violin's body,
ready to resonate with the sounds of your Kingdom,
eager to have Jesus' fingers touch us
to keep us in tune,
and longing to play the harmonies of your love
so that all who have ears may hear.

Harvey Richardson

403. Gracious God, equip us with the gifts of the Spirit
      and through the support of our local church,
      that in everything good we will be able do your will.
      We dedicate our lives again to share with you
      in the saving of the world for the sake of Jesus Christ.

Kenneth Todd, Ireland

404. Grant, Lord, that as we put our hands together in prayer,
      we may point to you,
      embrace the world
      and clasp our neighbours. Amen

Michael Wearing

405. Grant us, O God,
      honesty in our thought,
      authenticity in our faith,
      integrity in our dealings,
      warmth in our relationships,
      imagination in our discipleship,
      and hope in all things,
      through Jesus Christ our Lord. Amen

Mervyn Willshaw

406. Walk as you go from here
      God is there before you.
      Walk humbly as you go from here
      the churches await your coming.
      Walk softly as you go from here
      for the Spirit is abroad in all the earth
      and the voice of the Spirit speaks
      in every place.

China (source unknown)

407. Show to us, O Lord, the heart of your Kingdom; a destiny which leads to a cross, a way which leads to the losing of ourselves, a mission that is sure and steady and a life through which you can reveal your glory.

Toyohiko Kagawa, Japan (1888-1960)

408. Creator God, you have made your people in wonderful variety,
and called us into the unity of one Body.
Help each of us to bring our gifts
and to value the gifts of others
that together we may glorify you and give ourselves
in faithful and loving service,
through Jesus Christ our Lord.

John Sampson

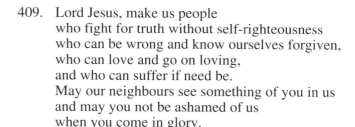

409. Lord Jesus, make us people
who fight for truth without self-righteousness
who can be wrong and know ourselves forgiven,
who can love and go on loving,
and who can suffer if need be.
May our neighbours see something of you in us
and may you not be ashamed of us
when you come in glory.

Christina Le Moignan

410. Living Christ, bring us from death to life:
from being the kind of church we try to maintain
to becoming a community of love,
and excite us with the truth: that to die and rise again
is the great mystery and challenge of the gospel
for each generation. Strengthen us through prayer
and give us courage to take the first step,
knowing that you, whose name is Emmanuel,
travel with us.

Maureen Edwards

411. Lord, we thank you.
Lord, give us vision.
Lord, give us wisdom.
Lord, we praise you.
Lord, give us a sense of wonder.
Lord, give us a sense of amazement.
Lord, lead us.
Lord, give us energy.
Lord, give us commitment.
Together we will carry the flame to spread your love.
Send us in Jesus' name. Amen

Methodist Association of Youth Clubs (MAYC)

Acknowledgements

We are grateful for permission to use material from the following writers and publishers. While every effort has been made to trace copyright owners, we apologise for any rights which have been inadvertently overlooked.

Caribbean Conference of Churches, permission sought   173

Christian Aid: *Bread of Tomorrow,* ed. Janet Morley   188

Christian Conference of Asia   301

Church Mission Society: *Morning, Noon and Night,*
ed. John Corden   104, 107

Denning, William C.   145

Edwards, Maureen   62, 109, 115, 152, 162, 282, 288, 317, 360, 410

Ethiopian Orthodox Liturgy (translated from Ge'ez by
Marcos Daoud). Originally published in English by the
Egyptian Book Press 1954   54

European Ecumenical Assembly:
Newsletter on the Second Assembly in Graz, June 1997   229

Fox, Peter   150, 156, 261, 263, 271

General Board of Discipleship, Nashville, USA:
Native American Leaders Make a Difference   217, 319

International Bible Reading Association:
Words for Today 1999   199
Words For Today 1998   253

Jasper, Tony   63

Lakin, Mark   154

Latin American Council of Churches   283

Leprosy Mission: *Prayer Handbook 1998*   178

Mead, Joy   321

Methodist & Presbyterian Churches of Aotearoa
New Zealand: *Mission Prayer Handbook*   269, 316

Index